W9-BXD-550

There Is No God

There Is No God

Atheists in America

David A. Williamson and George Yancey

ROWMAN & LITTLEFIELD PUBLISHERS, INC.
Lanham • Boulder • New York • Toronto • Plymouth, UK

Published by Rowman & Littlefield Publishers, Inc.
A wholly owned subsidiary of The Rowman & Littlefield Publishing Group, Inc.
4501 Forbes Boulevard, Suite 200, Lanham, Maryland 20706
www.rowman.com

10 Thornbury Road, Plymouth PL6 7PP, United Kingdom

Copyright © 2013 by Rowman & Littlefield Publishers, Inc.

All rights reserved. No part of this book may be reproduced in any form or by any
electronic or mechanical means, including information storage and retrieval systems,
without written permission from the publisher, except by a reviewer who may quote
passages in a review.

British Library Cataloguing in Publication Information Available

Library of Congress Cataloging-in-Publication Data

Williamson, David, 1955–
There is no God : atheists in America / David A. Williamson and George Yancey.
pages cm
Includes bibliographical references and index.
ISBN 978-1-4422-1849-9 (cloth : alk. paper) — ISBN 978-1-4422-1851-2 (electronic)
1. Atheism—United States. I. Yancey, George A., 1962– II. Title.
BL2747.3.W55 2013
211'.80973—dc23
2012047052

♾️ The paper used in this publication meets the minimum requirements of American
National Standard for Information Sciences Permanence of Paper for Printed Library
Materials, ANSI/NISO Z39.48-1992.

Printed in the United States of America

Contents

1 Understanding Atheism in the United States   1

2 A Brief History of Atheism   17

3 Who Are the Atheists?   33

4 The Foolishness of Religion   49

5 Progressive Politics as a Tenet of Atheism   65

6 Toward an Atheist Morality   85

7 Atheism in the United States   99

8 Summary and Conclusion   113

Appendix 1: Open-Ended Questions Used in Online Survey   125

Appendix 2: Interview Schedule for Atheists   127

Notes   129

Bibliography   139

Index   143

Chapter One

Understanding Atheism in the United States

Atheism, the affirmative belief that *there is no God* (and usually no supernatural as well), has been around since religion has asserted that *there is a God*—which essentially comprises all of recorded human history. Its message and who self-identifies as an atheist, however, seem to have morphed over the ages, depending on the religious beliefs of the day and the relationship between religious and political leaders. Because atheism always seeks, according to Gavin Hyman,[1] to negate religion, then the form and message of atheism changes over time to counter religious influences. In this book, after briefly reviewing the history of atheism and its relationship to existing variations of theism, we will hear from contemporary atheists, in their own words, what brought them to believe there is no God and what maintains and rationalizes that position. We will also listen to their attitudes toward religion in general and toward conservative or evangelical Christianity in particular, paying attention to the justifications they use to support their attitudes. We also will explore how those attitudes translate into political ideology and action. The voices of atheism, though relatively few in number, recently have grown and had a disproportionately large impact on important issues of our day, such as the separation of church and state, abortion, gay marriage, and public school curricula. As those voices increase, it is essential that we understand how and why those who are defined by such a simple phrase as "nonbelievers in the existence of God" should have such social and political influence.

While most of us have read or read about very recent and assertive atheists such as Christopher Hitchens,[2] Richard Dawkins,[3] Victor Stenger,[4] and Dan Barker,[5] little is known about the thoughts and convictions of everyday atheists, a shortcoming that we will in some small way address. Some may be

1

assertive in the spirit of those atheistic authors just mentioned—who recently have been called atheistic fundamentalists[6]—and some may be less assertive while still positing a belief of nonbelief, or what others[7] would call *positive atheism*. Others are content to simply not believe, to not assert an affirmative belief.[8] Regardless, although atheists of all stripes comprise only a small fraction of the U.S. population, they appear as a group to have grown in size and influence over the last half century and now have a surprisingly loud voice in American culture and public discourse.

Contemporary atheism in the United States gained national attention in the 1960s through the voice of Madalyn Murray O'Hair, the prototypical fundamentalist atheist. In her address to the Eighth Annual Convention of the American Rationalist Federation in 1962, she described the basic struggle of atheists throughout history as a "ceaseless struggle against ignorance and superstition."[9] She went on to emphasize the materialism that is central to atheism and the struggle against those who have ruled societies throughout history from a basis of ignorance and superstition made to sound rational through the guise of religion. So from at least that time, atheism has been publicly expressed as an affirmative belief in materialism that counters what atheists believe is ignorance and superstition.[10]

We will discuss this in greater detail later, but as we narrow the focus on those atheists who verbally and assertively express their nonbelief in God, we should keep in mind the fact that the more radical and outspoken have been the public voices of atheism as well as religion all along. Popular opinion in the United States, where religion is still quite robust, and where believers overwhelmingly outnumber nonbelievers, tends to favor religion of almost any kind over atheism, although as progressive ideology has grown, atheists find that among progressive religious people they at least share some common ideas. Atheism does run counter to popular opinion, but due to the fact that some from the Religious Right have attempted to influence political processes in ways that concern religious progressives, atheists may be experiencing a greater sense of inclusion than has been the case in previous periods of American history. The public messages from both extremes are usually expressed in combative and derisive language, a topic to which we will return in chapter 4.

Before we begin, it is important that we more clearly define who we are considering atheists for the purposes of this book. As we will discuss in the next chapter, there has been a good bit of confusion over terminology and an evolution in the meaning and use of various references to nonbelievers. That confusion is evidenced by the findings of the Pew Forum on Religion & Public Life, which found that only 5 percent of Americans reported that they did not believe in God or a universal spirit, among whom only 24 percent called themselves atheists.[11] This is substantially lower than the percentages yielded by other studies. Assuming the Pew figures are somewhat accurate, by interviewing only those who self-identify as atheist means that we probably have a sample of individuals who are committed to their nonbelief. For the purposes of this book, we are not interested in those who are not willing to openly self-identify as atheists, or those who report that they are agnostic—that is, that they do not know if there is a God and really don't think there is a way to know.

We also are not interested in those who report that they are not a member of any religious group, sometimes called the "nones." They may be religious, or spiritual, but they don't affiliate with any religion. Between 1990 and 2008 those who self-identified as none increased by 42 percent in the United States.[12] That's worthy of study, but for our purposes we are only interested in a subset of nones: those who believe, without reservation, that there absolutely is no God and no supernatural. According to an analysis of General Social Survey data from 1988 to 2000, approximately 14 percent of nones are actually atheists.[13] According to one study, atheists made up only 5 percent of nones but grew between 2001 and 2008 by 56 percent. It appears that many who are technically atheists do not self-identify for various reasons, including the fear of recrimination or marginalization.

According to figures compiled by Phil Zuckerman, atheists in the United States make up between 3 and 9 percent of the total population, ranking the country 44th in the proportion of the population who are atheists when compared to other countries. The countries that top the list are predominantly in Northern and Western Europe (led by Sweden, with a population between 46 and 85 percent atheist) and in Asia (led by Vietnam, with a population 81 percent atheist).[14]

From Zuckerman's figures we find some interesting fodder for debate. First, this is the type of data that scholars have used to refute the secularization hypothesis, which existed in some form as early as the seventeenth century and gained momentum through the late twentieth century. The hypothesis (which some call a theory) is that as societies modernize, they become less religious. Data indicating that one of the most developed countries in the world ranks only 44th in terms of the proportion of its population who are atheists clearly does not support that hypothesis. Second, the growth of atheism in a society that is, by world standards, quite religious indicates that there probably is conflict between these belief systems and evolving positions and arguments used by religion and its antagonists.

The estimates of the number of atheists in the United States vary from study to study depending on sampling methods, wording of questions or use of terminology, and other unknown reasons. For example, some studies may assume that someone who reports no belief in a supreme being or universal spirit is an atheist without directly asking, "Are you an atheist?" What we do know is that, although they are a relatively small minority, atheists appear to be growing in number and in their willingness to be identified as atheists and to voice their nonbelief.[15]

Over the last generation something has changed in the worlds of atheism *and* religion in the United States that makes us take notice. Not only is there a new atheism emerging that is forceful and unapologetic and a parallel increase in people who self-identify as atheists, but at the same time there appears to have been a surge in conservative religious affiliation and political action. Granted, the overall numbers and percentages of the population who self-identify as atheists are still relatively small, but the sheer rate of increase is worthy of investigation. With the data we have available we cannot say if or how much the increase in nones has been associated with the number of atheists. It could be that there is a whole continuum of people in the United States who are moving away from religious affiliation and belief and moving at least in the direction of the ultimate rejection of religion—the affirmative identification as people who do not believe in God, gods, or the supernatural. What we do find, however, is that those who self-identify as atheists also embrace science and, for many, a strong belief in the innate goodness of humans, or humanism.

The new atheism has been attacked by believers as well as, surprisingly, nonbelievers and atheists. As Jeff Nall points out, all atheism can specifically say is what atheists *do not* believe.[16] Those who go further in attempts to define what atheists *do* believe (such as the late activist Madalyn Murray O'Hair) he calls, oddly, "fundamentalist atheists." Narrowly speaking, "fundamentalism" is a term coined by and exclusively descriptive of a counter-evolutionary and counter-progressive movement in the early U.S. twentieth century to emphasize the fundamentals of Christian belief.[17] But even allowing Nall to use the term more broadly, fundamentalism describes an approach to the basis of belief, not disbelief. We are interested in all atheists, not just those who are assertive in their beliefs, such as materialism, and certainly not *just* those who would fit into the category of fundamentalist atheists. The only qualification is that they self-identify as atheists.

In addition, there have been changes in the American religious profile, especially over the past fifty years but more particularly over the last decade, when the pace of change and secularization seemed to increase. Those rather dramatic increases in nones and atheists have occurred as mainstream[18] Christianity has declined in the United States. In 1990 it was estimated that there were more than 14 million Methodists in the United States. By 2008 that number had decreased to 11.3 million. Similar patterns were observed for Lutherans, Presbyterians, and Episcopalians.[19] During that same period, more conservative denominations, including Catholics, Baptists, and Pentecostals, showed significant growth. This trend can actually be traced back much further, as Dean Kelley observed in attempting to explain why conservative churches are growing at the same time that liberal (progressive) churches are declining.[20]

We are not attempting to address why conservative churches are growing and progressives ones declining, but we do intend to answer the broader question of this apparent polarization of the religious and nonreligious dimensions of American society, especially the new assertive atheism. Both conservative denominations and those who report no religion at all, including atheists, are increasing—in some cases dramatically. The religious fear the moral decay of society as secularity and progressive rationality threaten traditional family values and moral structures. As the Religious Right has worked aggressively to influence politics and public discourse, progressives have countered with separation-of-church-and-state protests and formal organization. The culture war, in fact, seems to be a war fought by the extremes of American society—the religious conservatives who aggressively have been attempting to, in their view, redeem and restore conservative values and morals, and progressives who are alarmed by the threat of theocracy and counter with their own forms of aggression, seeking to elevate rationality and science over the myth of religion and religious control.

Paul DiMaggio and his colleagues found no evidence for a general polarization of American social attitudes except in the cases of abortion and political party affiliation from the 1970s to the 1990s.[21] However, they were looking at social attitudes, not specifically at religious attitudes. Political affiliation may mask the changes occurring in religious attitudes as progressive religion has declined, the number of nones and atheists has increased, and conservative religion has grown. It also may be true that there is strong polarization among some of the population who are deeply committed to the ideals of either end of the conservative-progressive continuum, while a majority of people who are not deeply attached remain in the middle.

Throughout this book we will look for other social factors that might explain this dramatic increase in those who self-identify as atheists, particularly in the American religious environment, as well as in politics and the experience and actions of those in other minority groups. Although atheists are most likely to be white and relatively well educated and affluent, in terms of their beliefs they are a clear minority, and to understand recent trends we need to see them in that light. Atheists do not need empirical studies to know that Americans in general do not trust them, just as African Americans need no tables or graphs to convince them that racism is alive and well in modern America. So while American atheists are, on the surface, well placed and privileged in American society, their disbelief marginalizes them in a society that has strong religious roots and a vigorous level of contemporary religious belief and involvement.

We obviously do not have to look far or think too hard to see what has transpired socially and politically in the last few decades among other minor-

ity and marginalized groups. Women, people of color, gays, Muslims, Hispanic immigrants, and others have clearly found a voice and have emerged to
begin claiming what they believe is their rightful place in American society.
From the suffragettes to women's liberation, from emancipation to the civil
rights movement, from stigmatized deviants to proud homosexuals, there are
no more apologies, no more resignation to the corners of society—they have
claimed a selfhood and self-respect enjoyed by the majority groups, despite
continuing discrimination from those within the majority who do not accept
their claims to normalization and equal status. Many of the atheists we interviewed for this book clearly expressed a sense of liberation from marginalization and a proud and assertive association with fellow atheists.[22]

Following the aggressive atheism of leaders such as Hitchens and Dawkins, they are more frequently "coming out," a phrase that the interviewees
used, not one that we have imposed while reflecting on their responses.
Billboards with atheistic proclamations can be found in most major cities,
invitations to join atheist groups can be found even in Muslim neighbor-
hoods, and marches with protesters carrying signs with coming out overtones
like "Hi Mom! I'm an Atheist!" are commonplace. A generation ago, most of
those people were tight lipped about their atheism because they knew the
judgment that likely awaited them. That reticence is understandable and not
without foundation. One recent study found that atheists in the United States
were considered the least trustworthy group when compared to Catholics,
Christian fundamentalists, Mormons, and even Muslims and gays. In the
1990s Americans were more likely to vote for a presidential candidate who
was gay or Muslim over one who was an atheist.[23]

But increasingly atheists are defying this alienation and proudly asserting
their disbelief. As one leader of a recent atheist rally in Washington, DC,
stated, "Private atheists need to come out because we want atheism to become commonplace."[24] Not only are they standing up for their nonbelief, but
the most radical are also, as mentioned earlier, atheistic fundamentalists,
accusing religion of controlling and even poisoning society.[25] In a more
moderate tone, in the seventeenth century, social philosophers such as Rousseau expressed the belief that Christianity, as it had been practiced in Europe,
actually distorted humans and human institutions. Rousseau, however, did
not advocate the eradication of religion, as did Hitchens, and chose instead a
new way of practicing civil religion.[26]

A (VERY) BRIEF HISTORY OF ATHEISM

In chapter 2 we will take a look at the history of atheism, particularly in the
Western world and its roots in Judaism and ancient debates from Greek and
Roman civilization on through to Christian history and contemporary de-

bates. For now we would like to just mention some highlights of that history to orient the reader to what we see as the most critical points in the history of atheism that shed light on its place and impact on current American culture and politics.

One of the first uses of atheism as a label came from classical and Hellinistic antiquity. According to Jan Bremmer, as early as the fifth century BCE the declaration by Anaxagoras that the sun is made up of molten metal—not terribly upsetting by today's standards—was, to Athenians who worshiped the sun as Helios the god, blasphemous.[27] However, later in the classical period it was even proposed that the gods and religion were created and perpetuated for the purpose of social control, something we will address at length later on, and soon after the life of Socrates we find the first use of the term *atheos*, or "godless," as a term of incrimination. At this point it appears that no one embraced the label, as it was only used to accuse and deride those without belief in the forms of religion that dominated the cultural landscape of that era.

The label "atheist" continued to primarily be used in derision, not for someone who was a complete nonbeliever, but for anyone *who did not believe in the accuser's God*. Bremmer refers us to the case of Polycarp of Smyrna, one of the most famous and beloved early Christian martyrs. Before being put to death he was instructed to say, "Away with the atheists," meaning, "Away with Christians who will not pledge allegiance to the Roman gods." In response the deeply religious Polycarp pointed to his accusers and proclaimed something to the effect of "Yes, away with the atheists," meaning those who did not believe in the Jewish/Christian God and his son, Jesus of Nazareth.[28]

By the seventeenth century in the West, atheism had become an acknowledged phenomenon although its adherents made up only a small part of society, mainly believed to be found among intellectuals.[29] It was also then first observed that atheism seemed to be linked to modernity and science.[30] As those became the most definitive characteristics of seventeenth- and eighteenth-century Western societies, so did the prevalence of atheism in a new form: it had within its ranks those who embraced the term proudly and began using "religious" as a term of derision, beginning with Diderot. No longer was "atheist" used to refer to someone who didn't believe in the God of the accuser; now it was used to refer to someone who believed in no deity at all. The lines began to be drawn, although at this time it was primarily in Paris and within the Roman Catholic world. People of reason began to voice publicly their dissatisfaction with the authority and dominance of the magisterium and the abuses of religion by the Catholic Church.

The history of doubt and its pioneers throughout history, particularly over the last four hundred years, has been celebrated by organizations dedicated to doubt and atheism. Authors such as James Haught[31] and Jennifer Hecht[32] have featured the profiles of prominent historical figures who decided against religion and religious control and spoke openly about their nonbelief. Similar lists are abundant on the Internet and are featured in publications from organizations such as the Freedom from Religion Foundation. From the ancients to the Enlightenment and all the way to American history and America's founders, the lineage of people who were bold enough to be public with their disbelief is long and impressive—certainly giving courage to contemporary doubters and atheists. According to Haught, what they all had in common was reliance on rationality, and in many cases a rationality that replaced religion with science as the ultimate source of knowledge and authority. This struggle over final authority on the matter still is at the center of the debate. Rationalists, materialists, and atheistic scientists (and those who rely on them for knowledge) complain that religion has no empirical proof of God or a hereafter. The problem with which they are left, however, is proving a negative. And the religious world has no empirical evidence that will satisfy materialists and rationalists. We will see these ideas, particularly a preference for scientific evidence and a belief in the innate goodness of humans, expressed very clearly in our interviews with atheists.

And there is strength in numbers and in association. At least one atheist organization can be found in most major urban centers. A soldier at a U.S. Army base recently organized an atheist rally to counter an evangelical rally that was dedicated to recruitment and conversion to evangelical Christianity. National and regional web-based communities of atheists have experienced exceptional growth over the last few decades, and that trend continues. This move-countermove pattern should not be surprising because religion and irreligion have been locking horns for millennia. If religion did not exist, there would obviously be no need for social organization of those who are not religious, which leads us to our first guiding principle.

THE DIALECTIC OF BELIEF AND DISBELIEF

A premise that will guide our discussion of atheism is that the voice and actions of atheists are shaped by the voice and actions of religion, as noted by Hyman.[33] Atheists seem to speak and act to negate the language and actions of the dominant religious voices of their culture and, therefore, are found engaged in the middle of the culture wars of recent decades. Perhaps we should not say the middle because, as we have already stated, the culture war seems to be fought from the ends of the spectrum of religious belief and nonbelief. But atheists have taken up arms in response to the perceived threats of the actions and words of the Religious Right. Before exploring the interviews conducted for this study, we will, in the next chapter, lay the groundwork for this premise by briefly reviewing the history of atheism to show how it has morphed through time, as has religion. It appears to be a type of dialectic with no synthesis in sight—only combative responses, parries, and thrusts. Each side may change, but it changes its message and strategies to counter the latest moves of the other. As Hyman points out, some argue that modern atheism has developed in response to unique, contemporary forms of theism that are quite different than those found in earlier periods of Christian history.

Hyman asserts that changes in the religious landscape have directly altered the position and voice of atheism at times in Christian history. For example, with the ideas of Duns Scotus (John Duns the Scot), a fourteenth-century Franciscan priest and theologian, God's difference from humans became ontologically altered from "other" to "more." God could be measured in the sense that God was, essentially, quantifiably *more* than humans (superhuman), not substantially *other*. The danger was that if this was so, atheists could argue that God should be empirically measurable and within the realm of reason. Needless to say, the inability of Christians to provide empirical support for belief in God, whether perceived as more or other, remained an empty argument for atheists and actually supported their position.[34]

Making this public dialogue even more complex has been the voice of those who assert that religion and science are *not* incompatible.[35] John Polkinghorne is one among many physicists and scientists who have made the positive assertion that one may encounter the cosmos with the very best eyes and mind of science and still believe in a God and a world that transcends this one.[36] In fact, their appreciation for the "awesomeness" of God is enhanced by their understanding of the nature and scale of the universe. When asked to defend their belief in explaining this world and human existence, some (though certainly not all) have used the argument of what has come to be known as intelligent design, or, roughly speaking, the idea that the unfolding of the universe and the development of human life on this planet has been and is being guided by one who is transcendent. Needless to say, this response has not been well received by atheists and is generally dismissed, as have all other attempts to make science and religion compatible.

ATHEISM, POLITICS, AND SOCIAL CONTROL

In this book we also explore the centrality of social control, primarily control of politics and public policy, usually as exerted by religion and opposed by atheists (and progressives in general). Peter Berger observed almost forty years ago that religion has been used throughout history as a means of rationalizing and justifying various forms of social control.[37] Civil authority and religious authority have historically been enmeshed, as each seeks to establish and enforce moral authority over populations. It is all about control. That is why the separation of church and state is so important to atheists and progressives alike. They share an opposition to those who would, on religious grounds, attempt to limit human liberties and impose religiously based legal and ethical constraints.

Jack Gibbs has made a compelling case that control is even the central notion of the entire discipline of sociology.[38] If he is right—and we at least are open to that idea—then the answers we are looking for may be found by orienting our analysis in that assumption. After all, war is about control, even the so-called culture war. In earlier eras, struggles for control resulted in open conflict and bloody wars. In more recent times we have developed more civilized ways of struggling for control through political processes. Contending parties attempt to structure society to fit their respective ideologies, whether through the strict separation of church and state or the Defense of Marriage Act (DOMA).

From the beginning of the discipline of sociology, it has been observed that society is a moral phenomenon, that it is ordered by structure and the rules and privileges that structure provides. In other words, without walls and boundaries, society cannot exist. The problem is that society creates the boundaries that it then must observe so that order is maintained. But what is the source of authority behind decisions to establish those boundaries? Max Weber argued that, in the West, rationality replaced traditional and charismatic forms of authority with those based on legal rationality.[39] Reason trumped tradition and religion, and, according to atheists, real social progress was made. As we have already mentioned, throughout most of Western history, religion and politics have been strange but frequent bedfellows. While conservative Christians do not see that as a problem (as long as they are in the democratic majority), progressives overwhelmingly support the separation of church and state and see rationality and reason as the only legitimate basis for structuring society.

Even within the history of Western Christianity this struggle could be seen as reason began to trump tradition. The protesters of the Protestant Reformation were, among other things, throwing off the control of the Vatican and its magisterial authority in favor of a less hierarchical church structure and a greater dependence on scripture and rationality to guide the church: no more arbitrary rules and doctrines coming from a distant Vatican that added to the burden of an already difficult life. The Catholics may have had their periods of scholasticism, but Protestants approached biblical scholarship as *the* way of obtaining correct guidance, throwing out the authority of the magisterium. *Sola scriptura* was the battle cry.[40] Therefore, with social control being the central issue, we can find it at work in the struggle between belief and nonbelief, as well as among contending factions of believers.

But once wholly centralized authority is abandoned, the question becomes, what is the *proper* and most rational form of organizing church authority? Some, such as the Anglicans, chose to simply decapitate the Roman Church and move to an episcopal model of leadership through a college of bishops. Others, like the Presbyterians, brought the lay community into authority structures, while others moved toward more local or congregational authority. Although most of these groups explain their organization on scriptural grounds, as sociologists we are more interested in exploring the sociological dynamics behind these various forms of structure. And one pattern we see is a move toward autonomy, or, in other words, freedom from external control and more local capacity to organize, believe, worship, and act. This, we believe, the religious and the nonreligious held in common; thus both were subject to broader cultural shifts occurring in Western societies.

Two parallel dynamics have characterized Western history: (1) a movement toward an emphasis on individual rights, and (2) a reliance on rationality rather than religion, myth, or superstition. We see these trends among believers and nonbelievers because both live subject to broader social influences. Atheists may say that science is all we have to go on, whereas modern religion embraces science to a certain extent, although ultimately ending with faith-based esoteric references to the ineffable existence of the supernatural and to one all-knowing supreme being.

Support for this argument can be found in research on religious preference and practice in the United States over the last half century. Since the 1960s there has been an interesting pattern in religious affiliation in the United States, something that sociologists call "religious switching."[41] A growing number of individuals report that the religion with which they affiliate as adults is different from the one with which they affiliated as teens (when most people identify with the religion of their parents). Loveland reported that approximately one-third of Americans practice a religion or are members of a denomination that is different from the one practiced in their family of origin.

From the most hierarchical form of religion in Roman Catholicism we have come to an era in which the individual has the capacity to be his or her own authority, choosing if and with whom to affiliate and whose moral structure to follow. The individual owns the right to self-determination in all matters religious. A bumper sticker of the 1960s intended for political motivation has become much more universally fulfilled: "Question Authority." For atheists, it appears that the authority being questioned and dismissed is *the ultimate* source of authority, structure, and constraint for believers: God. In the sociological sense of the term, both atheists and believer activists who attempt to control public discourse can be regarded as sectarian and fundamentalist in the broadest sense of the word.[42]

We have found that a majority of atheists replace faith in God with reliance on science and on innate human goodness, or humanism. Many describe themselves as free thinkers, supporting our control argument that what they are doing in part by embracing disbelief is freeing themselves from the capacity for any human institution, especially religion, to tell them what to think or feel. Unburdened by religious myths, fears, and imaginations, they are emancipated to engage the world with a reasoning mind. For many atheists, that means embracing science and empiricism as the only real alternative.

If we bring in Max Weber's notion that the guiding force behind the development of Western ways of thinking and organizing was and is rationality, then we see some of the sources of conflict in the relationship between religion and irreligion. Rationality and scriptural authority were elevated over magisterial and traditional authority in most of the Protestant movements. However, they all—at least in their original forms—embraced a view of scripture as authoritative and the means by which God exerts authority over human behavior and organization. Most contemporary atheists claim rationality and science as the arbiter of what is real and what is not, of what is authoritative and what is magical thinking. In their view, there is no magic, and the only real mysteries are the things we do not yet know empirically.

For many believers, this may seem a dismal thought—that there is no mystery, that there is no "other," and that there is no eternal father to protect and comfort them. For many nonbelievers, though, the idea is liberating: no fear of death and no fear of judgment, just a marvelous universe to experience and explore—empirically.

Another bit of evidence that control is central to this issue can be found in the life and work of Hubert Henry Harrison, a black intellectual from what is known as the Harlem Renaissance of the early twentieth century.[43] Harrison ferociously opposed Christianity as a white man's religion based on a racist document—that is, the Bible. The Bible nowhere directly condemns slavery and even endorses it, though in places proscribing slave owners' actions toward slaves. It provides a theodicy of despair for oppressed blacks, urging them to seek an eternal reward and not to hope for one in this lifetime, the same theodicy it provides for all who are marginalized in the existing structures of society. Don't rock the boat, be humble and obedient, and after you die you will have eternal rewards. That logic is probably similar to the logic used by peasants during the Toltec period of Mexican history. Those peasants were put to work erecting great religious monuments and then, convinced that it was for the good of society that they voluntarily offer up their lives on those same monuments, they allowed Toltec priests in collaboration with civil authorities to cut out their hearts.[44]

The contemporary struggle between atheists and conservative Christians, although usually expressed in rational or theological/philosophical language, is ultimately a struggle for control of the valuable resource of political influence. Each camp has its own ideas as to when and how it is appropriate for government to intervene in defining social policy, and each has a moral and social agenda. Through political systems and processes, both atheists and conservative Christians define the role of government to meet those agendas, not because either atheism or conservative religion is necessarily political in nature, but because these groups, as do all groups, seek to draw moral boundaries in ways that favor their worldview. In a sense, they are both engaging in social and moral gerrymandering.

In the contemporary debate we see both anti-religious and religious groups attempting to influence cultural and political processes. The emphasis in this study is on the attitudes of atheists who overwhelmingly want a strict separation of church and state and a dampening or demolition of the influence of religion on public life. We should also keep in mind the concerns of the religious that the anti-religious are the ones with too much influence, already bringing about a dismissal of religion in public discourse. Stephen Carter refers to this as the trivialization of religious devotion, or the relegation of religion to social and political impotence, which he observed almost twenty years ago.[45]

THE DERISION OF RELIGION AND BELIEVERS

A common characteristic of atheism is its criticism of religion and people who are religious, especially religious leaders. Sometimes that criticism is simply dismissive, and sometimes that criticism is derisive and intentionally sharp. We will explore this pattern and attempt to find the reason and intent of such criticisms in chapter 4. Several observations should be made at this point regarding the criticisms we heard from our samples.

Regardless of the date, dominant religion, or level of modernization or scientific sophistication, atheists have been equally dismissive or derisive of religion and those who espouse religion. From ancient Greece to eighteenth-century France and certainly to twenty-first-century American culture, there has been a deep chasm between religion and atheism. In successive eras during that long history there have been variations on a theme: Religion seeks to order society through an untestable set of beliefs and dogmas, while atheists counter with a reliance on reason and empirically testable hypotheses and a materialist view of the cosmos. And of course, then come the counter-counterattacks by the religious who are equally dismissive or derisive of nonbelief. Despite our historic pluralism, Americans have always been dismissive and suspicious of atheists, and atheists know this better than believers. Many, if not most, atheists have feared having their nonbelief made public. It was only with the influence of Darwinism in American academia, including its seminaries, that religion began to feel the pressure to defend itself beginning in the late nineteenth century and, as mentioned earlier, with the founding of what is now called Christian fundamentalism in the early twentieth century.[46]

This so-called dialectic between scientific evidence and religious tradition and ideology is not a true dialectic, just as two arguing individuals who are set in their ways cannot have a constructive dialogue. Each may alter their opinion or arguments over time not to find rapprochement with the other but rather to find more convincing arguments for their own beliefs—or disbeliefs. While, as mentioned earlier, there are those who are attempting to bridge science and religion, the people at the extremes of the public debate will probably be the last to be moved by such efforts.

This conflict has often been elevated to a fever pitch, costing lives and fortunes and social status. There is a great deal at stake—the ultimate definition of meaning and being and, if it exists, eternity. In the Christian tradition made infamous by Dante and often used by Christians in attempts to control the behavior of others, believing or acting outside the moral boundaries or established teachings of the church may bring *eternal* punishment.[47] To buy into the dominant religious views of the day, people throughout the history of Western Christianity either had to behave or deal with the knowledge of impending doom. John Lennon's song "Imagine" is sounding better and better, as are materialism and the belief that Dante had a distorted vision of an imaginary place. It is not hard to understand why some who have been raised under that threat may have opted for a less transcendent and more materialist view of reality.

We found an interesting difference in how opinions about religion, especially evangelical Christianity, were expressed by atheists in two different parts of our inquiry. In the first, we conducted an online survey distributed to membership lists of organizations that are either expressly anti-religious or advocates of a strict separation of church and state. We were able to select out those who self-identified as atheists and analyze their answers to open-ended questions about conservatives and evangelicals. A vast majority of the responses were dismissive of religion in general, and most were insulting and derisive of evangelical Christianity. Criticism ranged from labeling the religious as delusional to labeling them as sexist, anti-scientific, or abusive.

In the second part we actually sat down in face-to-face interviews with atheists, approximately half from the Midwest and half from the Southern Bible Belt. In face-to-face interviews, the atheists were certainly dismissive but clearly not as virulent as those in the online survey. More of them were willing to say that there is room in the world for the religious if only they will keep it to themselves and certainly not try to influence political processes or educational institutions and curricula. And they would say, by the way, stop trying to proselytize the world. Believe if you like, but leave the rest of us alone.

At their harshest, atheists may dehumanize those who are religious or consider them throwbacks to earlier evolutionary cousins of humans. Particularly in the online survey, atheists commonly referred to those who are religious as developmentally impaired, brutish, or unevolved.

Finally, the level and nature of the dismissal or derision of religion by atheists may be influenced by personal experience with religion. For that reason, we decided to test this hypothesis by interviewing atheists in the Bible Belt and in a Midwestern location with a reputation for progressive thinking. We will discuss our findings later, but for now we want to focus on a variation of what is known as the contact hypothesis: more contact and interaction with others who are different from you will alter your attitude toward them. As one of us has found, increased contact with people of other races and ethnicities may have a positive influence on how one views the "other."[48] However, if that contact is overwhelmingly negative, the influence may be in the opposite direction. The most obvious assumption, based on the contact hypothesis, is that atheists in the Southern Bible Belt will feel more constrained about publicly expressing their disbelief and will be more negative toward evangelical Christianity. Likewise, atheists in a progressive Midwestern setting may lean more toward being dismissive of religion and less toward derision. Of course, personal attitudes vary depending on personal experience, and just because an atheist lives in a conservative religious area does not mean that of all his or her personal interactions with conservatives will be negative.

AN OVERVIEW OF WHAT FOLLOWS

The themes outlined and briefly discussed in this chapter will be more clearly articulated in the following chapters, which have been organized to help the reader clearly understand the nature of what we are attempting to do, the sociological ideas that guided it, and the most important findings. We begin with a brief history of atheism to set the stage for a better understanding of contemporary American atheism. Again, this history is not exhaustive, but rather a summary focused on the guiding principles of this study, primarily the relationship between religious and atheistic ideologies and how they have each attempted to discredit the other in different ways, at different times, and under very different social and political circumstances.

In the third chapter we explore the profiles of our respondents, both those from the online survey and those with whom we conducted face-to-face interviews. As mentioned earlier, although they are a marginalized group, atheists also belong to groups that are considered privileged. American atheists tend to be white, well educated, and relatively affluent and older in age. We explore why we believe this is the case, and how that profile combined with their atheistic assumptions influences their attitudes toward broader social and political issues.

From there we take up the consistent expression of dismissal or derision of religion by American atheists. It is here that we explore the validity of contact theory, looking into exposure to and experience with evangelical Christians. One issue that we will deal with is the virtual world of the Internet. Many of these individuals get much of their ideology from virtual communities and through Web-based information. To the extent that this is true, then perhaps we will find little support for contact theory, although we would argue that personal experience tends to be more influential than blogs or Internet postings.

In chapters 5 and 6, respectively, we take up the issue of how atheists express themselves through political activity and how they construct and maintain structures and systems of morality that are not based on revelation or religious tradition. We have already noted that many American atheists express a deep and abiding confidence in innate human goodness, although most do not articulate why that is the case. Regardless, both political action and systems of morality have one thing in common: the control of culture and social structure. What boundaries must we observe, who establishes those boundaries, and by what authority do they do so? For atheists, it seems that rationality grounded in basic humanism is the answer. Anyone who uses religion to create or enforce boundaries that atheists consider irrational is the enemy.

In the concluding chapters we provide an overview of American atheism informed by the analysis of this study and other available scholarship on the subject. And we will attempt to address some summary questions, including those that we posed earlier in this chapter. Just how common is the dismissal and derision of religion expressed by atheists? On what basis do they say what they do about religion and those who are religious? How central does social control seem to be as a latent or manifest motivation behind atheists' attitudes and political activity? How are we to understand the worldview of atheists and their motivations in political action and public discourse? Are the current trends likely to continue or has the recent upturn in the numbers of self-identified atheists been an anomaly? Finally, is there any hope for rapprochement in the relationship of atheism and theism?

Chapter Two

A Brief History of Atheism

Another exhaustive history of atheism is neither needed nor intended here, only a summary view that highlights our main premises of the dialectic of belief and nonbelief, the centrality of political and cultural control, the influence of science and empiricism on the nature of both atheism and religion, the particularly derisive nature of many atheists toward dominant forms of religion, and the characteristics of contemporary American atheists, their organization, and their message to a largely religious society. [1]

Our attempt to understand contemporary American atheists requires that we understand them and their messages as situated in a long history of debate over belief, contending beliefs, and nonbelief. The growing voices of modern atheists did not erupt suddenly in response to Jerry Falwell and the Moral Majority or Pat Robertson and his attempt to influence the political process or what many perceive as his blaming the victims for attributing Hurricane Katrina to the immorality of New Orleans. Their battle cry was not solely in response to Pat Buchanan's declaration of a culture war at the 1992 Republican National Convention. As there has been an evolution (perhaps that is not the best word, but it is descriptive) of religious beliefs and expression over the centuries, so has there been a mirrored evolution of atheism and its beliefs and expressions. Atheism seeks to negate religion; therefore, the message of atheism must adapt to the message of religion as expressed and practiced specific to time, place, and culture. [2]

As with any organism, when societies or particular social groups are threatened they are energized for fight or flight. In this historical debate it primarily has been fight. As we argued in the first chapter, the emerging American culture favors, for the most part, the ideal of the inclusion of marginalized groups[3]—that is, with the possible exception of atheists. That being the case, atheists are coming out and are countering conservative

Christian attempts to, in the words of many of our respondents, move us backward at a time when we have made so much progress and there is a great promise of more. The threat of repealing this progress is intolerable and threatening to atheists who have just come to a place where they are beginning to feel empowered to speak out against religion and for a just and civil society of inclusion.

In order to set the stage for our study of contemporary atheists' ideas and beliefs, we will begin with a brief review of belief and atheism, first in ancient Jewish history and then in the three phases outlined by Bremmer: the classical, Hellenistic, and Roman-Christian.[4] With the lessons from that review, we will then explore the history of atheism in recent American history, particularly since the late nineteenth century, when progressive ideologies, fueled by evolutionary theory, began to influence American universities and seminaries.

ATHEISTS IN JUDEO-CHRISTIAN HISTORY

Believers and nonbelievers have been around since the beginning of recorded history, although the term "atheist" can only be traced back to the fourth or fifth century in Greece. Prior to that in most civilizations the issue was not so much *does* a person believe, but in what God or gods does he or she believe? Certainly the citizens of Ur of Chaldea (in modern Iraq) from which Abraham came were religious, but they were not believers in his monotheism. The ancient Egyptians are famous for their elaborate forms of religion, including worship of Ra (Re) the sun god and the divinity of the goddess Nut and her daughter Isis. All of the civilizations destroyed by the Hebrew conquest of Canaan had their gods as well, as did the continuing enemies of Israel, including the Assyrians, Babylonians, Persians, and eventually Greeks and Romans. The question typically was not "Is there a God?" It was more often "Whose god is most powerful?" Evidence was provided by who won battles and wars. The political battles were not motivated by religion, but were interpreted using religious imagery.

There are few references to atheism in Hebrew scriptures, and those that do exist are not absolutely clear in their meaning, although there is no doubt that they are stated with contempt by religious Israelites. Both Psalms 14 and 53, traditionally attributed to King David, begin "Fools say in their hearts, 'There is no God.' They are corrupt, they do abominable deeds; there is no one who does good."[5] However, it is not clear that the reference is to people who in the contemporary use of the term could be considered atheists—that is, materialists. It is possible that the reference is to those who do not believe in the Hebrew God. At the very least these passages lead us to believe that nonbelievers were suspect, doing evil and not reflecting the goodness of the Israelite God.

In a quick online search for biblical references for "godless," we were surprised at first that the earliest mentions (not in chronology, but in order as organized in the Christian Old Testament, not the Tanakh) of the "godless" were in the book of Job. Job and his three friends, Bildad, Eliphaz, and Zophar, who have come to console and advise him in his affliction, all make frequent references to the godless as those who forget God and who are barren, evil, wicked, unjust, empty, and soon forgotten. These are intended to contrast the godless with Job, who has, up to this point, been a believer in and follower of God. As in the references from the Psalms, however, it is difficult to know if these are actually nonbelievers as atheists or those who ignore God and who cannot count on God for help. The latter is more likely considering the almost universal religiosity, however measured, of cultures of that time.

In Isaiah 9:17 reference is made to the evil of the godless, referring in part to the Philistines who had inflicted so much damage on Israel. It is well known that the Philistines were religious, primarily worshipers of Dagon, a god of fertility, so "godless" here clearly does not mean "atheist" in the materialist sense. In fact, we found no evidence that "godlessness" in the Hebrew scriptures is ever intended to imply materialist atheism as much as to accuse those who followed other gods or wicked Hebrews who did not take God and the law to heart. In other words, they had forgotten God and fol-lowed their own desires, which led them into evil.

CLASSICAL, HELLENISTIC, ROMAN AND EARLY CHRISTIAN REFERENCES TO ATHEISM

The origins of the concept of atheism as it is currently used can best be found in the classical history of ancient Greece. The pantheism of Greece and later of Rome were well established and commonly followed by citizens. The multiple gods were linked to the many dimensions of nature and natural forces and included such well-known beings as Zeus, Atlas, Aphrodite, Eros, Apollo, and, last but not least, Hades, the king of the dead (or the under-world). As mentioned in the first chapter, during the classical period and into the Hellenistic period of Greek history, the assumption was that everyone was religious, although each citizen might have a preference for some gods over others. [6]

The materialist observation of Anaxagoras mentioned in the first chapter was new to a world that had been, to that point, overwhelmingly theistic about interpretations of natural phenomena. Even for the most conservative contemporary evangelical Christians who have learned to adapt theology to natural science, that is not a problem. But for those who counted Helios among the divine in this relatively pre-scientific era, it was blasphemy. Although others had been outspoken in attempts to redefine divinity, apparently none had made such a materialist claim that, in fact, that big, shiny disk in the sky is actually just glowing, red-hot metal. Although the term "atheist" was not in use at the time, Anaxagoras would have been ridiculed for not believing in the divinity of this supreme element of nature. We apparently do not know if he maintained belief in any of the other gods, but his rejection of the divinity of Helios clearly placed him in the camp of the godless.

The period of the early Greek philosophers, from Anaxagoras to Socrates, became over time the period of natural philosophers who regularly were derided in Greek comedies as well as tragedies. However, natural philosophy prevailed and by the end of the fifth century BCE, the sophist Prodicus identified the source of religion in the forces and substance of nature.[7] The gods of agriculture, particularly bread and wine, were elevated when humans learned that from grain humans could make bread, and from grapes they could make wine. Thus the emergence of Demeter and Dionysos, gods of bread and wine, allegedly based on historical figures who discovered bread could be made from grain and wine could be made from grapes and who, upon their deaths, became deified. This is one of the first hints we have that some humans attributed the gods to human imagination.

By 430 BCE the natural philosopher Bellerophon began one of his plays with "Does someone say there are indeed no gods in heaven? There are not, there are not, if a man is willing not to rely foolishly on the antiquated reasoning."[8] Clearly rationality had already been established as a counter to religious belief by that early date. Later in that passage Bellerophon makes another observation that is echoed in contemporary atheistic messages: People who quietly and obediently live religious lives are easily exploited and controlled. The powerful know that and use it to their full advantage. Bellerophon also engages in denigration of the religious who rely on "antiquated reasoning," a trait we found common among American atheists.[9]

Other philosophers of that era showed signs of natural philosophy and were persecuted, including Diagoras, Euripides, and Socrates. Only later, by the mid-fourth century BCE, do we find in Plato the term "atheist" (*atheos*) in reference to those who were godless and were without belief in or reverence for gods. Most who were considered *atheos* were sophisticated intellectuals who were well educated and considered people of high social status. We will find later in the profiles of the atheists we surveyed and interviewed what we already have claimed—that modern American atheists are people of relatively high status and educational achievement, and many of the "new atheists" most vocal in their movement come from intellectual or academic circles. For now, we should keep in mind that rationality, derision of the religious, and the accusation that the powerful use religion to control the weak are central to the atheistic argument, whether in fourth-century BCE Greece or twenty-first-century America.

By the time the Greeks (Seleucids) conquered Israel and the second Jewish Temple was defiled by Antiochus Epiphanes ("the gods' beloved") in the second century BCE, religion was still strong and commonly practiced and atheism was mostly found in intellectual and philosophical circles. One Orthodox Jewish source characterizes Epiphanes' motivation as a desire to impose godlessness on the Jewish people. [10] As we earlier observed, this does not mean literal godlessness but rather the abandonment of traditional Jewish religious belief and practice in favor of pantheism. The second-century BCE Maccabean uprising at least temporarily halted the Seleucid efforts to impose Hellenistic religious and social customs on the Jewish people and allowed a temporary return to temple worship in Jerusalem.

ATHEISM IN LATER ROMAN AND EARLY CHRISTIAN HISTORY

With a few modifications, the pantheism of the Greeks translated nicely to the theology of Rome, with the later emergence of the emperor himself as a deity. Among other motivations to conquer the world for Rome was the elevation of the mission to divine status, and all of those conquered by Rome were expected to at least pay lip service to the emperor and the gods of the Romans. Religion was one with the state and used as a rationalization for the domination of the strong over the weak. The weakened Jews, long since in Diaspora, were soon overwhelmed by the Romans, who had grown tired of their pesky resistance. The Second Jewish Temple was finally destroyed by Rome in 70 CE. Roman persecution of the Jews, often rationalized by religious and empirical allegiance, ultimately led to the forceful destruction of Israel. Once again, political and national interests coopt religion to justify the forceful exercise of violence in order to control.

But just before that final insult, we should note the visit of the Apostle Paul to Athens, the historic center of Greek philosophy and learning, during one of his missionary journeys probably in the decade before Jerusalem's fall. As a Roman citizen he had status and traveled freely, and on this visit, as recorded by physician/historian Luke in the New Testament Book of Acts (17:22–23), Paul publicly addressed the Athenians, beginning with "Athenians, I see how extremely religious you are in every way. For as I went through the city and looked carefully at the objects of your worship, I found among them an altar with the inscription, 'To an unknown god.'"[11] So we at least have evidence that the Athenians were highly religious even after being conquered by the Romans, and this was perhaps made easier by the shared pantheism of the two cultures. Paul, a faithful Jewish Christian, chose to appeal to the Athenians' religiosity rather than to derisively call them godless as the word was used in Hebrew scripture, perhaps a decision based on his mission to evangelize and not alienate.

Although Paul was rather gentle in this example, Christians early on began to use the term *atheos* with derogatory intent when addressing or referring to one who was pantheistic. It was their refusal to recognize pantheistic deities and especially the divinity of the emperors that led to the Roman persecution of Christians during Christianity's first three centuries.

To this point we see an evolution of "atheist" from accusatory references to "godlessness" (although not in the materialist sense) to a description of those who advocate materialistic explanations for natural phenomena without divine association, to an accusatory reference for anyone who does not believe in the accuser's God. The latter was apparently the most common use of *atheos* throughout most of the rest of the first millennium after the rule of Constantine in the fourth century CE. With little change in Western Christianity over that time, there also was relatively little change in the presence or voice of atheists.

By the time of Thomas Aquinas in the thirteenth century CE, the term was still used in that latter sense. However, things began to change in Christian theology.[12] Aquinas had argued that references to God and God's characteristics were merely analogous, not literal. God was qualitatively different from humans, holy, or "other." By the fourteenth century we can see an apparently subtle shift in the works of John Duns Scotus, a Franciscan priest and scholar.[13]

Duns Scotus,[14] as he is customarily called, advocated a natural theology that made no ontological difference between the nature of God and of humans. Humans differed from God only in magnitude or quantity, not in essence. God was domesticated and made to be like us except more, not other.[15] To some this was almost heretical, but over time it became a part of the fabric of Christian theology. What those theologians did not realize was that this gave atheists a new means of attacking Christian belief systems. Religion had been brought into the realm of reason and, therefore, of science. Hyman's point is that as Christianity changed, it basically set itself up for new attacks from a modified atheism. These new attacks needed to challenge the existence of God but on turf closer to home. Rather than having to argue against a being that was wholly other, atheists began to argue against the existence of the ultimate superhuman. The groundwork was laid for the empirical question "Where is the scientific evidence for the existence of this God?" However, it took more time for science to develop before it began to provide a basis for atheistic questions. And as science gained more credibility in the broader Christian society, so it was further strengthened in its ability to debate God's existence using a language that most people eventually understood.

This may be part of the reason for a later shift in the relationship between science and religion. Until the seventeenth century there had been relative harmony between the two, largely based on the strong influence of Aquinas's marriage of Christian theology and Aristotelian philosophy. Science remained a branch of philosophy, and human reason was thought to be capable of understanding the moral, ordered nature of the universe.[16] That the world exists means that something must have been the original, intentional mover of matter, a conscious being capable of making the universe work and who created it to operate by moral laws and principles. In some form, theism prevailed even though beyond the "unmoved mover" argument it still had no scientific evidence to show.

Until the sixteenth century, Roman Catholicism was basically the only game in town for those who identified with and practiced religion in Western Europe. Of course, Jews, Muslims, and those of other, smaller religious traditions were represented but in such a minority that they had little impact on the religious landscape for much of that time, with the exceptions of Muslim encroachments in Spain and from the eastern Ottoman Empire. Aligned with the state, Catholicism ruled most of Western Europe.

That tells us something important about the atheism of the day. If, as Hyman argued and as we maintain in this work, atheism in any age is the attempted negation of religion, then its characteristics may be explained by the nature of Western Roman Catholicism of that time. What was it about Roman Catholicism that atheists believed needed to be negated? One answer is power and the abuse of power, often reflected in the practices of monarchies enmeshed with religious authorities. If atheism had no new argument about the nonexistence of God, it certainly had (and has) something to say about the abuses of religion and its distortion of fundamental human goodness.[17] Humanism gained strength as an alternative to religion.

Even the religious of the day observed and often objected to the abuse of authority by the Vatican. Martin Luther's complaints were aimed at ecclesiastical reform (hence, Reformation) and were not for the purpose of establishing a new branch of Christianity. If religious objections to the church's abuse of power ended in the greatest rift in Christian history, then what would be the effect of nonbelievers' revolt against religious control, especially as it was aligned with political power? With the philosophical development of rational ideals for governance, combined with the exponential growth of science and rational reliance on empirical observation over superstition and tradition, the effects were dramatic and the aftershocks are still being felt today. Using rationality and science, progressive atheism could take down oppressive political structures by undermining their religious foundation.

The rift of the Protestant Reformation also introduced a new problem: pluralism. As Berger observed, pluralism often leads to relativism, and relativism *may* be a slippery slope to at least agnosticism, if not outright atheism, or a return to a normative form of religion.[18] So conflict over control within Christianity and especially Protestant Christianity may have set it up for fresh attacks from atheists.

This movement began at a time when there was a serious intellectual battle going on in Western Europe, sometimes called the "Battle of the Books" (in England) or the conflict of the "Ancients and the Moderns" (in France). In many ways that conflict was very similar to the culture wars we are experiencing in modern American history.[19] Progressive intellectuals emerging from the Enlightenment advocated social progress based on rationality (what Weber would later call legal-rational), while traditionalists advocated loyalty to established social structures and forms of authority. Although the debate was conducted primarily in intellectual circles and within academia, it reflected real changes that would eventually lead to the American and French revolutions, to democratic forms of leadership, and to devotion to science and empiricism as the primary ways of knowing.

The Enlightenment represented to Kant a growing up of humans, a coming of age—the Age of Reason.[20] Moving into the eighteenth and nineteenth centuries, it meant a rational, scientific approach to learning about humans, our societies, and the world and the universe we inhabit. Although some influence of Romanticists such as Rousseau was felt, the orientation toward feeling and intuition was overshadowed by the Age of Reason. During the Enlightenment we also first see "atheist" used as a self-descriptor by Diderot.[21] He was not the first atheist, but he was among the first, apparently, who had enough confidence in science and reason and enough disdain for religion that he was willing to publicly announce his nonbelief.

It was also in the late eighteenth and early nineteenth centuries that modernism was again linked with atheism. The end product of the rational progress of modernity was believed by many to be atheism.[22] There was an ongoing attempt to reconcile differences and put an end to the science-religion split, none of which fully satisfied the strongest representatives of either side. Some attempted empirical efforts, such as Locke, while others attempted a philosophical solution, such as Kant, who argued that we must place God beyond the human intellect, not within.[23] In other words, he was promoting a theology that reversed the influence of Duns Scotus by making God other, not just more.

Early sociologists such as Comte argued for a positivist vision for society, one that was ruled by reason and positive science. They were highly critical of the abuses of religious authority and the foolishness of basing social organization on the fantasies of the religious. The Enlightenment thinker Baron d'Holbach, an eighteenth-century French author, philosopher, and encyclopedist, as well as one of the first outspoken atheists in Europe, argued that "all religion is an edifice in the air; that theology is only the ignorance of natural causes reduced to system; that it is a long tissue of chimeras and contradictions."[24]

By the mid-nineteenth century, science was booming, explaining more and more of the natural world and its phenomena that traditionally had been given religious explanations. Thomas Huxley, among others, although known as a strong advocate of Darwin's evolutionary theories, was not completely comfortable with the label of atheist and so coined a new term, "agnostic," which at least allows for the possible existence of God, although declaring that there is no empirical way to know. Others, such as George Holyoake, preferred the name "secularist."[25]

Darwin himself, uncomfortable with the implications of his own theories yet struggling with the idea that a beneficent God would allow such suffering in a world that he created, wrote,

> I am inclined to look at everything as resulting from designed laws, with the details, whether good or bad, left to the working out of what we may call chance. Not that this notion at all satisfies me. I feel most deeply that the whole subject is too profound for the human intellect. . . . Let each man hope and believe what he can.[26]

Darwin's doubts about God's existence, primarily due to his observation of suffering in the world, were also central to the doubts of John Stuart Mill, who took religion seriously but was never religious for that reason (among others). Despite Darwin's concerns, his commitment to science and scientific method compelled him to move forward and, eventually, challenge the beliefs of many in the Western world.

ATHEISM IN NINETEENTH- AND TWENTIETH-CENTURY AMERICA

We do not want to wade into waters that might easily distract us from the purpose of this book, but we do want to generally describe religion in the beginning of American history and set the stage for the influence of progressivism and Darwinism in the late nineteenth century. What is important to establish is that, in the beginning, the rule of the day for settlers in the New World was religious intolerance, not tolerance. Certainly many came who sought the freedom to worship according to their convictions, but the idea of religious pluralism was not what they originally had in mind. The original colonies were closely aligned with specific denominations and typically formed either a theocratic or totalitarian form of government. The idea of separation of church and state had not been introduced and was not central to the original ideals of our earliest populations.

It was only as the colonists faced a common threat that they forged the idea of a federal government and ideas of a shared culture. And so important was the issue of the relationship of church and state that responding to that matter became the subject of the very first constitutional amendment. In the First Amendment, all that is really said regarding religion is that Congress shall not appoint an official national religion and shall not impede the free exercise of religion. States were free to do so and did. At the state level, there was no expectation of a separation of church and state.

What developed from this was not a melting-pot Christianity or a strong ecumenical movement, but rather a general notion of what it means to be a Christian by which Protestant denominations developed a vision for the newly unified nation that would provide a common ethic and morality. [27]

This "common Protestantism," as Hunter calls it, was challenged by Catholic and Jewish immigration from the late nineteenth into the early twentieth centuries. Protestant pluralism was a much easier pill to swallow than living and working side by side with followers of a pope whom some believed to be the anti-Christ, or with descendants of "those who killed Christ." But no one was prepared for the ultimate challenge to religiosity in the United States in the form of progressive, scientific ideology and the evolutionism of Darwin and Huxley.

As had apparently always been the case, atheistic and progressive ideas were most commonly found in intellectual circles and within academia. And so it was in academia, including seminaries that had traditionally prepared ministers for service primarily in what would now be considered fundamentalist denominations, that these ideas first took root. The predicament that confronted scholars of that era was whether to follow the rational logic of science or continue believing in a religious worldview that more and more seemed to be merely myth and tradition rather than historical fact.

In 1861 the occupant of the "Perkins Professorship of Natural Science in Connexion [*sic*] with Revealed Religion" at Presbyterian Columbia Theological Seminary was James Woodrow, uncle of President Woodrow Wilson. Woodrow was both a theologian and a scientist who found himself in a position that forced him to take sides or come up with his own way of reconciling Darwin's theories and data with Presbyterian theology, which up to that time had been quite conservative. His response was that evolution was divinely guided but the human soul was immediately created. [28] In other words, Darwin is right, but at just the right stage of evolution God created souls in the human species, thus making them qualitatively, as opposed to naturally, evolved creatures. *Now humans were other, not just more.* This took place during the Civil War, and the General Assemblies of the Presbyterian Church, U.S. (Southern) did not ratify Woodrow's position until 1969, more than one hundred years later. Of course, by that time Presbyterians had been so influenced by progressive thought that they already were ordaining women to the ministry.

Another seminary professor, Alexander Winchell, was fired from his position at Vanderbilt Divinity School (Methodist) after publishing a work in which he argued that there had been a pre-human race, the "Pre-Adamites," who had preceded humans in the evolutionary process. At the time Methodism in the United States was still a very conservative denomination, and altering scriptural histories to accommodate Darwin's evolutionary ideas was unacceptable. But as with the Presbyterians and the seminaries of many American denominations, progressive ideology slowly took over and is now the norm. Fundamentalism is out.

By the early twentieth century, progressive ideals had permeated much of American academia, which had long been the case in Europe. If God had not yet been domesticated, at least religion had. There are even some who claim that Europe had never been as religious as most have assumed. Some have argued that it was the separation of church and state and the diminished role of religion in establishing and upholding moral standards that *revealed* Europe's irreligiosity rather than caused it.[29] The fact that most of Europe is now nominally religious at best, they argue, is not support for secularization theory but a historical condition that was made manifest when the cloak of religion was removed.

While the French Revolution had given credibility to atheism and discredit to religion, the opposite effect was felt in Britain, where atheism became associated with "immorality, lawlessness, and far-left revolutionary politics."[30] The American experience sided with the British although it was somewhat different, with religion being exercised more purposefully in the working and lower classes while progressive ideals, including evolution, were gaining acceptance in American academia (including seminaries) and intellectual circles. The independent, pragmatic, working-class ethos that built the U.S. economy and society was, for the most part, shaped by religion.[31] This, according to Hofstadter, set the stage for what he called anti-intellectualism in America, the distrust between what (biblical) common sense and traditional values told us and what was coming out of the mouths of intellectuals. Man from apes? And apes from slimy ooze? And all of this by chance? What are you, a communist?

In fact, it wasn't long before atheism became closely linked with communism; therefore, atheists and other intellectuals were suspected of being anti-American. The line was long and filled with intellectuals and progressives—many of whom were atheists—waiting to be questioned during the McCarthy hearings, showing that by mid-century these associations were felt at the highest levels of our government.

American society "was a society of courage and character, of endurance and practical cunning, but it was not a society likely to produce poets or artists or savants."[32] It also was a society whose values had little need for the intellectual or, for that matter, the highly educated. Intellectuals are useless to a pragmatic people trying to tame the land and build industry. Who needs critics who sit on the sidelines and abstract everything, including (and most importantly) the highly valued history and morality of the Bible?

This curious history resulted in an association of terms for a large part of the working American middle class: intellectual-communist-atheist. They are obviously not synonymous, and there are obviously loyal capitalists who are atheists as well as believers who believe in socialist and/or communist ideals, and intellectual scholars in even the most conservative religious denominations. But in the first half of the twentieth century, all of these terms were suspect and atheists, knowing they were in a very small minority, tended to stay safely within their academic and intellectual circles, even though progressive ideas were being disseminated by clergy who, trained in more progressive seminaries, began to popularize progressive ideas within America's most prominent churches.

Before we look into the developments of atheism in the United States since the time of McCarthyism, it is important for us to mention again the conservative Christian attempt in the early part of the twentieth century that was intended to be a countermeasure that would preempt this progressive takeover of American religion and culture: the development of Christian fundamentalism.

In reaction to this threat of progressive ideology and Darwinism to conservatives' foundation of biblical literalism and inerrancy, a movement was created to reinforce the fundamental beliefs of the Christian Right. A series of publications, *The Fundamentals*, published between 1910 and 1915 and funded by conservative and wealthy elites, gave a name to the new movement.[33] The energy of this movement was fueled by both the existing and cyclically renewed anti-intellectualism already present in American society and the fear that Darwinism and biblical higher criticism were undermining traditional religion, which was, the conservatives believed, the bedrock of American society.

Intellectualism and Progressivism as applied to Christian teachings (e.g., James Woodrow) yielded, in their opinion, an emasculated religion that voided Christianity of its most substantive beliefs and took down the moral barriers by which America had, in their perception, obtained the blessings of God and held back the floodwaters of materialism and immorality. Relegating the Bible to myth or allegory opened a door for atheism's advance. Now that these progressive ideas were alive *within* Christian seminaries and churches, atheists finally had a much greater opportunity to go public with their message, to live with their nonbelief as openly as Christians had always been able to live.

So the stage was set within the first half of the twentieth century for what by 1992 became labeled a culture war, and among leaders on the progressive side of that war there were and are many atheists who now forged a message aimed at Christian fundamentalism and political activism.

ATHEISTS ORGANIZE FOR ACTION

Atheism in the United States has not organized into a single institution, but the influence of atheism can be seen in the establishment of other institutions that hold to atheistic ideals such as the limitation of religious authority, strict separation of church and state, and individual rights. After World War I and the Bolshevik Revolution, fearing that communist sympathies might be brewing in the United States, Attorney General Mitchell Palmer began rounding up and deporting suspected radicals in 1919 and 1920. These became known as the Palmer Raids, and they outraged progressives who were open to alternative forms of government and ways of thinking about economics and human rights. Legal efforts to defend and protect the targets of the Palmer Raids formed what was to become the American Civil Liberties Union, or the ACLU.[34]

The ACLU shortly thereafter partnered with Clarence Darrow in the famous Scopes Trial of 1925. Concerned that the Tennessee legislature had passed a law banning the teaching of evolution in public schools, the ACLU recruited John Scopes to do just that in order to test the law. Despite their efforts, Scopes was found guilty (although the verdict was later overturned), but the story had made national headlines and brought into public consciousness the apparent standoff between religion and science, at least as it had to do with evolution.

Subsequent causes added to the ACLU's image and activity, including opposition to World War II Japanese internment camps, the 1954 joint victory with the NAACP in the *Brown v. Board of Education* case, and perhaps their most famous win in the 1973 *Roe v. Wade* case, which was argued before the U.S. Supreme Court. According to their website, the ACLU currently has around one hundred staff attorneys who work with approximately two thousand volunteer attorneys, handling almost six thousand cases every year. The ACLU is funded by foundation and individual charitable gifts. No government funds support its efforts. Its mission is to defend the constitutional rights of every American, primarily freedom of speech, the right to equal protection under the law, due process, and the right to privacy. They particularly strive to serve the underserved, including women, people of color, lesbians, gay men, bisexuals and transgender people, prisoners, and people with disabilities.[35] The humanism of the ACLU's philosophy and mission, along with the elevation of individual human rights over religious ideals and the moral codes of traditional Christianity, have developed over time a perception that everyone in the ACLU is an atheist. We do not know the percentage of those who work with and for the ACLU who are atheists, but the ACLU has provided support for atheists' right not to be subject arbitrarily to religious controls and traditions. In that respect, atheists are treated the same as any religious group.

In 1963 Madalyn Murray O'Hair started American Atheists, an organization that worked for the absolute separation of church and state. However, unlike Americans United for the Separation of Church and State (now American United), one of American Atheists' primary purposes was the defense of atheists, at the time a quite controversial position considering the conservative spirit of the day. O'Hair was one of the first and most vocal positive atheists who wasn't content with simply not believing: she preached an affirmative belief in materialism. Of course, without religion there would be no need for such a position or organization. Today American Atheists, the organization founded by Madelyn Murray O'Hair and the organization that most explicitly defines atheism as a central belief and reason for being, has one hundred local affiliates across the United States. It works with those affiliates to spread the message of atheism, provide educational opportunities for those who desire a more intellectual foundation for their atheism, and support the cause of civil rights. [36]

The Freedom from Religion Foundation (FFRF) began in 1978 with similar sympathies for atheists and today is the largest free thinkers organization in the United States. By "free" they mean freedom from the undue influence of religion and the liberty to live and act without the cultural or institutional restrictions of traditional religion. This position puts them squarely in the tradition of the French *philosophes* who, centuries before, advocated human progress without the impediments of religious influence.

Although the public voices of the Moral Majority and Christian Coalition have subsided somewhat since the Reagan administration, interest and membership in progressive organizations have not. In 2005 membership in FFRF was approximately 6,000. By 2007 that number had almost doubled, reaching 11,600. In 2009, FFRF reported a membership of 14,084, an astounding 235 percent increase since 2005. From a mere three members in its first year, FFRF has grown into a national group with representation in every state and in Canada. [37]

Soon after FFRF was started, famed television producer and author Norman Lear founded People for the American Way (PAW) in 1981 as a nonprofit organization "dedicated to making the promise of America real for every American: Equality. Freedom of speech. Freedom of religion. The right to seek justice in a court of law. The right to cast a vote that counts. The American Way." [38] They list as their focus "Progressive advocacy" through media attention and direct appeal campaigns. Again, the percentage of PAW workers who are atheists is not known, although the extent to which they have worked to limit the ability of religious groups to impose themselves and their values on broader society leads us to believe atheism is not uncommon in their ranks.

As we have stated from the beginning, atheism has an interesting and long history that morphs depending on the religious spirit-of-the-day and the extent to which religion, on its own or in collaboration with the state, constrains civil rights and human freedom. The contemporary American picture is complex, with the influences of progressive thinking encroaching on traditionally conservative religious institutions, with traditional religion in a defensive posture as it perceives the erosion of fundamental Christian beliefs, and with a polarization at the extremes of atheists and believers, progressives and traditionalists.

In the following chapters we will allow self-identified atheists to express themselves as they reveal what motivates them, what concerns them, how and why they feel as they do about religious conservatives, and how they view political processes and those who attempt to control them.

Chapter Three

Who Are the Atheists?

While there is evidence that the percentage of atheists in the United States is growing, this is still a small group. In a report that otherwise documents the emergence of individuals without traditional religious beliefs, at least one study found that self-identified atheists only make up less than 1 percent of the individuals in the United States.[1] The small size of this group makes it difficult to study since it becomes somewhat tricky to find enough respondents to do meaningful analysis. To conduct useful quantitative analysis of atheists, it is necessary to collect data from a large number of potential respondents. For this reason, conducting a useful quantitative investigation is not feasible.

However, given the dearth of our present knowledge about atheists, there is still much work that can be done in developing a qualitative understanding of this group. Qualitative analysis can inform us about the patterns of thought that are common among atheists. Furthermore, such work can provide us with testable ideas that can be substantiated or refuted in future empirical work. Even though we cannot automatically generalize our findings to all atheists in the United States, we are still taking another important step in our understanding of this subculture.

In this chapter we will discuss the methods used in our examination of atheists. Although we do not have a representative sample, the use of multiple qualitative methods provides us with a breadth and depth of data that is very informative about atheists. We will explore some of our early findings about atheists to understand the basic context in which members of this group make sense of their beliefs. Using some of these findings, we further investigate the directions our research will take in the upcoming chapters. We end this chapter with an initial assessment of atheists' perspective and experience in the United States.

METHODOLOGY

To investigate the attitudes of atheists in the United States we collected data with two distinct, but related, research efforts. First, as part of a larger project to examine cultural progressives,[2] we conducted a survey of those who state opposition to the Christian Right. We located several organizations that had as one of their primary missions resistance to the Christian (or, in some cases, Religious) Right. Members of such organizations are supporting institutions that have made one of their primary causes the limitation of the influence of the Christian Right.[3] To conduct the research, we sent a link to the survey to the leaders of the organizations. Those leaders then sent the link out to their members. The open-ended questions in the survey can be seen in appendix 1.

For the sake of privacy, the names of the organizations remain confidential. However, two of the organizations possess a national scope while another is located in a Southern state. This last organization skewed attempts to assess the regional distribution of individuals who resist the Christian Right. A fourth source of respondents came from a contact in a small organization. The contact spread the survey to members of other smaller organizations and provided us with further respondents. When we finished collecting our data, we had 3,577 respondents. Of these, 2,483 respondents answered at least one of the open-ended short-answer questions. We clearly do not have a probability sample. But we do claim that we have obtained a sufficiently large sample with which we can reasonably locate patterns within those with significant antipathy toward conservative Christians.

The sample provided us with an abundance of individuals who self-identified as atheists. It did so for a couple of reasons. First, atheists are a natural enemy to organizations attempting to increase the political influence of religion in society. As we will see from some of our findings, one of the fears atheists have is the infusion of religion into politics. Thus, atheists are more likely to seek out organizations that oppose a political entity such as the Christian (or Religious) Right than are other individuals. Second, one of the major organizations we utilized has as its primary purpose the general resistance of religion. We anticipate that this organization likely artificially increases the number of atheists and agnostics in our sample. As a result of these factors, we ended up with a sample in which atheists made up 61.7 percent of the sample. When we removed the non-atheists from the sample, we still had 1,786 respondents, of whom 1,451 answered at least one of the open-ended short-answer questions. We will examine our responses for patterns that, we argue, are likely to be present among atheists in general, although we will not be in a position to explore how common these patterns are among atheists. Ideally, future quantitative research will provide scholars with the ability to determine the generalizability of our findings.

To augment our understanding we also analyzed the primary literature we collected from organizations dedicated to supporting atheism. We subscribed to two of the organizations and received a hardcopy version of their newspaper. We also received e-mailed updates from one of the organizations. We read and analyzed this information to provide ourselves with primary source material from atheists. This material is even more important than normal because, as we will later argue, atheists receive a lot of their knowledge about their worldview from the writings of other atheists. We looked for common patterns in how the writers of the articles and letters to the editor[4] in this material perceived atheists, religion, criticisms of atheism, and larger society. This content analysis is key for seeing how the leaders of these organizations want to represent atheism to the larger society. As such, this material provides valuable information about the vision atheist organizations have for our society, their defense of atheism, and how they understand the place of atheists in the United States.

The literature generated by these organizations is available for public consumption. One of the reasons for this literature is to recruit potential atheists to the organizations. Another plausible reason for this literature is to promote a favorable image of atheists to non-atheists. Naturally the leaders of these organizations strive to paint themselves, and atheists in general, in the best possible light. There may be a social desirability effect in that the leaders will focus on only positive aspects of atheists and atheism. We fully acknowledge this possibility. Yet how these organizations attempt to create this positive image is a valuable way of learning how atheist leaders perceive themselves. Such leaders undoubtedly will forward arguments that they believe will be persuasive to potential new members of these organizations. There are certain values that atheists are more likely to appeal to that are in keeping with their perception of reality. Since the leaders are atheists themselves, they are in a position to understand the type of concerns that other atheists may have. So looking at the image that leaders of these organizations attempt to portray in their literature is insightful regarding how they perceive themselves—even if it is an overly idealized perception.

Finally, we wanted to talk to atheists directly. We conducted face-to-face interviews of atheists in two different areas of the country. One of the areas was in a Midwest college town where progressive values, and not traditional religiosity, tended to dominate the local political atmosphere. The other area was in the South and known for its strong religious culture. The areas were chosen to contrast the perspective of atheists who live in an area where their atheism is generally supported with the perspective of atheists who live in an area in which atheism is treated with more suspicion. Since atheism is generally less supported than other religious orientations,[5] we believed it to be important to understand how atheists may alter their perspective when they feel more potential threats from religious majority groups.

We interviewed twenty-six atheists in the Midwestern area and twenty-five from the Southern metropolitan area. We used local atheist organizations to gain the names of potential respondents. The organization in the Midwestern town has more of a national reputation than the local organizations we used in the Southern city. This may skew some of our results, as different types of atheists may join contrasting types of organizations. But the strength of such an approach is that any findings documented in samples from both places are likely to be relevant to atheists in different areas of the United States. In the Midwestern area, the organization announced our project and contact information. That allowed the atheists to contact us. In the Southern metropolitan area, we used snowball sampling techniques to increase the number of atheists for us to interview. We relied less on formal organizations to make initial contact but instead found a few individual atheists through those groups who then directed us to other atheists. The interviews in that area occurred over a couple of months while the interviews in the Midwestern town occurred over only a week of time. However, we believe that such a difference in the time frame of the interviews was unlikely to affect our results.

The interviews generally lasted anywhere from a half an hour to an hour and a half. The average length of the interviews was forty-three minutes. Our goal was to learn about how individuals became atheists, what their logical justification for accepting atheism was, how atheism contributed to their overall well-being, and what they feared about religion. The interview schedule can be seen in appendix 2.

Our first few questions were designed to assess the events that occurred to lead the individuals toward atheism. The presupposition behind the questions was that atheism is a philosophy that individuals develop within the course of their lives. Such a presupposition is in keeping with some of the primary and secondary literature[6] that describes atheism as a choice made by rational consideration. Atheism as a philosophy accepted at some point within the course of the respondent's life was most often the case, but some individuals indicated that their atheism was a part of their lives from the very beginning. It was almost as if they were born atheists. The questionnaire then explored how atheists perceive the benefits of their atheism and whether they have ever had any doubts about it. We ultimately closed the interviews by more fully exploring how atheists perceive religious individuals and what the ideal society for the respondent would be in regard to religion. Such questions may not directly address why individuals become atheists but they can indirectly assess their motivations by exploring how atheists characterize those with whom they disagree.

We freely draw on these three sources of primary data (survey, interviews, and primary literature). It is our intention to treat them somewhat equally as sources of information, although the interviews allowed us to

Table 3.1. List of Interview Subjects

Name	Age	Sex	Education
GY1 John	46–60	Male	Some college
GY2 Ben	Over 60	Male	Master's Degree
GY3 Rick	18–30	Male	Master's Degree
GY4 Jennifer	18–30	Female	Bachelor's Degree
GY5 Bill	46–60	Male	Master's Degree
GY6 Betty	Over 60	Female	Some Graduate
GY7 Don	31–45	Male	Bachelor's Degree
GY8 Ethan	31–45	Male	Bachelor's Degree
GY9 Timmy	31–45	Male	Bachelor's Degree
GY10 Shirley	31–45	Female	Doctorate
GY11 Dan	Over 60	Male	Master's Degree
GY12 Henry	46–60	Male	Some College
GY13 Mickey	46–60	Male	Some College
GY14 Ralph	Over 60	Male	Master's Degree
GY15 Allison	Over 60	Female	Bachelor's Degree
GY16 Jack	Over 60	Male	Doctorate
GY17 Teresa	Over 60	Female	Master's Degree
GY18 Kyle	Over 60	Male	Bachelor's Degree
GY19 Nick	46–60	Male	Some Graduate
GY20 Paul	Over 60	Male	Some College
GY21 Abraham	Over 60	Male	Doctorate
DW1 Nicole	Over 60	Female	Master's Degree
DW2 Frank	31–45	Male	Bachelor's Degree
DW3 Albert	31–45	Male	Doctorate
DW4 Riley	31–45	Male	Some Graduate
DW5 Barbara	46–60	Female	Bachelor's Degree
DW6 Horatio	46–60	Male	Doctorate
DW7 Isaac	18–30	Male	Some College
DW8 Lenny	46–60	Male	Some College
DW9 Bruce	Over 60	Male	Master's Degree
DW10 Tom	46–60	Male	Bachelor's Degree
DW11 Debra	46–60	Female	Bachelor's Degree
DW12 Victor	Over 60	Male	Some College

SS1 Marsha	18–30	Female	Some College
SS2 Jan	18–30	Female	Master's Degree
SS3 Matt	18–30	Male	Some College
SS4 Alexander	31–45	Male	Some College
SS5 Leroy	31–45	Male	Bachelor's Degree
SS6 Edith	31–45	Female	Bachelor's Degree
SS7 Butch	31–45	Male	Bachelor's Degree
SS8 Richard	31–45	Male	Some Graduate
SS9 Ramon	Over 60	Male	Master's Degree
SS10 Jimmy	46–60	Male	Some College
SS11 Sam	31–45	Male	Doctorate
SS12 Wilma	31–45	Female	Bachelor's Degree
SS13 Bernard	31–45	Male	Master's Degree
SS14 Orlando	31–45	Male	Some College
SS15 Francis	31–45	Female	Master's Degree
SS16 Judy	31–45	Female	Some Graduate
SS17 Peter	18–30	Male	High School
SS18 Elaine	18–30	Female	Some College

obtain the most direct answers to many of our questions. For some points, the interviews may be more important than the other sources of data. However, we expect that the primary written literature generated by atheist organizations is going to be shaped by the needs of the organization to make an attractive presentation to other atheists, interested non-atheists, and even critics of atheism. Thus it is a different but valuable source of information for us to draw from. When we can substantiate points with data from all three sources, it will obviously strengthen the argument that a given perspective is quite common among atheists. However, we contend that because of the subtle, but real, differences between these sources of information that we utilize, it is unrealistic to expect most of the contentions in our study to be supported by all three sources. As such, we are not concerned when some of our quotes utilize only one or two of these sources.

As we report the data, we run into a dilemma due to the differing sources of data. Typically, pseudonyms are attached to data collected by interviews. We will continue this tradition. The pseudonyms, along with a brief demographic explanation of each respondent, can be seen in table 3.1. This was not feasible with the data collected from our online survey. Given the sheer number of respondents to that survey, we simply ran out of fairly common names. As we discuss those respondents, we will do so with a brief demographic description of the respondent. Thus the reader will be able to tell if we are discussing an interview respondent or a respondent to our online survey by whether we use a pseudonym or a brief demographic description as we present the information from that respondent. The themes from each collection of data are basically the same; however, the different questions used help to produce some variation in the answers between the two groups.[7] Finally, we want to guard the identity of the secondary sources that we used in this research. We will alert the reader that a statement comes from a secondary source so that we do not create confusion where there is neither a pseudonym nor a demographic description next to a statement.[8]

WHO ACCEPTS ATHEISM?

In later chapters we will spend more time looking at what the atheists have to say as to why they became atheists and their perceptions about religion. But for now there is value in exploring some of the demographic and social features that are found in our data about atheism. We found the atheists from our online sample to be 72.6 percent male, 93.8 percent white, and 48.9 percent over forty-five years of age. A total of 40.2 percent had a graduate degree. We found among our interview respondents a sample that was 70.6 percent male, 86.3 percent white, and 49 percent over forty-five years of age. Of these, 35.3 percent had a graduate degree. In addition to our samples, which are admittedly not random, there is other evidence about the demographic characteristics of atheists. According to the 2007 Baylor Religious Study, atheists are 63.3 percent male, 96.4 percent white, and 35 percent over the age of fifty. Of these, 23.7 percent have a graduate degree. Furthermore, 24.2 percent of the atheists in the Baylor Religious Study made more than $100,000 a year, indicating that atheists are more likely to be wealthy than other Americans. We did not measure income but have confidence that our sample generally matches the general demographic trends of atheists in the United States, although the degree to which atheists are more likely to be male, white, older and highly educated differs from the Baylor sample.[9]

It is with a high degree of confidence we can argue that the typical atheist in the United States is a highly educated, wealthy, older, white male. These are all qualities that indicate an individual who is in a majority group position in society. There is no denying that even with its relatively recent gains in social status, atheism is a religious belief[10] that has minority group status. However, the individuals who adhere to this belief tend to have majority group status in other social dimensions. A quality connected to the acceptance of atheism is the possession of majority group status in most, if not all, of the other social dimensions of inequality.

It becomes reasonable to consider why possession of majority group status may be conducive to the acceptance of atheism. In the next chapter we will see evidence that atheists tend to argue that their beliefs about religion come from a rational exploration for truth, as opposed to the irrationality of religious out-groups. Majority group status can feed into the confidence atheists have about their ability to make determinations about social and theological reality. It is reasonable to speculate that because the respondents enjoy majority group status, they have been encouraged to think of themselves as being in a superior position to understand reality. They are well educated and wealthy, which may help them to have confidence that they have access to proper training and information. They are older, male, and white, which may indicate that they have been given a great deal of deference in their lives. Such confidence may help them to hold onto atheist beliefs in a society where such beliefs are still a minority opinion.

However, there is another way in which majority group status may help to substantiate atheism. It is possible that this status has insulated them from many of the societal problems that plague their peers. As a result, they perceive little need to seek help from external sources, whether those sources are supernatural or not. Since they have little need for such aid, they feel free from the desire to seek out religious comfort and are less likely to subscribe to religious beliefs. If this scenario is accurate, then many of the needs that religion offers to believers are simply not attractive to individuals with major societal advantages. The theme of being responsible for oneself without the help of external support was one that was stated quite a bit in our face-to-face interviews of atheists.

> If you don't have God in your life, you won't be a good person because these eyes watching you just like Santa Claus know when you're good and when you're bad. I'm not a perfect person, but I try to be a reasonably good person, and I don't need somebody watching me to make me that way. So I didn't feel that I needed, I didn't feel I needed the comfort. I didn't feel I needed the explanation, and I didn't feel that I needed the guidance. (Betty)

> I think I rely more on myself than the idea of waiting for some divine power to come in and make everything all better. I realize I have to do something. I need to go out and make something happen. (Jennifer)

Linked to such an assertion is the perception of religion as a crutch. Some atheists perceive religion as something that aids weak individuals. Not all atheists with such a perception were negative in this application of their perceived purpose of religion. Some of them saw religion as preventing some individuals from doing a great deal of damage to others in society. However, atheists tend to envision themselves as not needing such a "crutch." They believe themselves to be sufficiently strong individuals to not have to rely on supernatural beliefs to be a good and healthy person.[11] Even though they have enjoyed the benefits of majority group status, some of them believe that the benefits they receive from their lives are the results of their own efforts and perspective on life. Several of the atheists we interviewed talked about relying on their own strength to get through the trials of life.

> If I was not a person who sees my life as being in my control and my happiness a result of my own effort, I would be terrified of the Christian Right because they are attempting to create a theocratic state where sacrifice is the standard of good and where selfish living is considered evil. (male, 26–35, some graduate school)

> As an atheist, you just know that, number one, there's no expectations that you need to follow, any rule that is not something that you can just rationally understand. So there's more responsibility. You can't just read a book and be told what to do. You have to actually think, so there is a pressure to be responsible for yourself more so than a Christian. You can't take solace in the idea that God will forgive me if I make a mistake. If I make a mistake, then it was just me being stupid; I should have known better. (Alexander)

> Ultimately, what I'm able to do with my life is my own responsibility, and not up to anybody else, or what God has to create my faith, or anything like that, I'm not sure if you wanna say support—sense of support, but at the very least, an acknowledgment that right or wrong, it's up to me. And I don't know if support is the right word, but at the very least, that understanding for me is a sense of strength because if I don't do it, who else is gonna do it for me? (Richard)

There is clearly a strain of individualism that is part of atheism. As we will later note, atheists do understand the importance of social structure in the shaping of people's lives. Indeed, we will show how atheists tend to argue that society has to change to aid those who are marginalized. But they paradoxically perceive an importance for the individual to take care of himself or herself without relying on supernatural help. Thus atheists have an individualist orientation as it concerns dealing with otherworldly support while they endorse a political orientation that seeks a collectivist approach to societal solutions.

We will deal more with the political aspirations of atheists in later chapters. But the individualist perspective toward otherworldly issues is vital to understanding why atheists support such aspirations. If there are no supernatural sources of aid, then aid must come from materialist sources. Since the social position of atheists situates them to enjoy material success, it becomes relatively easy for them to see that success as the result of their efforts and fortunate position in society, instead of otherworldly intervention. If atheists tend to believe that their success is linked to their own efforts, it becomes evident that the reason other individuals are not successful is because of their marginalized status and because those individuals are living out a fantasy.

Atheists then can envision marginalized individuals coping with their failure by turning to religion to help them deal with their own and societal inadequacies.

> If something bad happens, there's—God or someone will watch out for me. I think a lot of humans really have that need, to believe that. (Henry)

> They tend to be more along the follower-type people who need something to believe in. They want someone else to blame for their problems and are generally quite intolerant as well as ignorant. (male, 18–25, some college)

> I think the best way to battle the religious Right is through economic development. I think this movement gets its fuel from poor, scared people. We need to fight this battle in the courts and legislatures, but we also need to provide middle-America with stable jobs and healthy communities. (male, 26–35, bachelor's degree)

Atheism, like other social philosophies, is linked to the social interest and position of individuals who have adopted that philosophy. Our contention is that certain philosophies meet important needs and concerns of individuals in certain places in society, and their ability to do so helps to explain why certain individuals are likely to be drawn to accepting those philosophies. Previous work has documented that the ways in which religion develops theodicies, or explanations for evil, tend to benefit the economic and social position of the religious group.[12] Likewise, atheists have developed explanations about supernaturalism that benefit their majority group status. We speculate that this creates an understanding of atheism that attracts individuals with majority group status. The accuracy of our initial speculations can be debated; however, it does seem clear that majority group status is linked to atheism.

It is also noteworthy that atheists are fairly likely to come from nonreligious or weakly religious homes. About half of the atheists interviewed (52.9 percent) came from homes where there was no religion or where religion was very weakly practiced. In many of those homes where it was weakly practiced, there was little or no attendance at religious services by the atheist's family of origin. About half (55.3 percent) of those we interviewed stated that they had never believed in the supernatural.[13] We counted those who stated some belief as a young child among those who stated that they had ever believed in the supernatural. This means that nearly half of all atheists stated that they had never believed in the supernatural even as a small child. A typical response comes from Don: "It just didn't make any sense to me. Just the concept that something cares whether or not I put on a button-up shirt and dress pants and sit in the stuffy room on a hard chair for an hour every week . . . I'd say I was an atheist before I realized what an atheist was."

This does not mean that there were not any former believers among the atheists. We did find some that even considered joining the clergy before becoming an atheist. Furthermore, Dan Barker is a famous atheist who used to pastor a church and authored a book about his transition that is widely read among atheists. However, it is fair to state that generally atheists come from a less religious tradition than non-atheists. Coming from such a tradition undoubtedly made it easier for some of them to embrace atheism since they could perceive it as a possible religious choice from a very young age.

For those who did, at some time, have religious beliefs, we found that attendance at a college or university could be an important mechanism by which they lost their religious beliefs. We found that exactly a third of those who at one time had religious beliefs lost their beliefs, at least in part, due to their experiences in colleges or universities. A typical story can be seen in the life of Bruce, who discussed his early religious beliefs: "As a child, I remember many a night of devotions in the living room, where we'd read the Bible and conclude with prayer on our knees next to the couch and everybody would say a little prayer of their own. So I grew up with pretty significant religious values in my family. I embraced those values." Although he accepted the values of his Baptist upbringing, this changed as he attended college. At that college he was required to attend two religion classes. It was here that his doubts begin to surface.

> It was my first time of having any experience with talking about concepts like demythologizing about the history of development of religions in the area where the Hebrews and Sumerians all were, you know? And I got fascinated by—you know, there's a number of creation stories out there and they're surprisingly similar in a lot of ways, where there are stories all over the place. It wasn't just what was in the Bible. And that began to get me to start thinking.

Bruce began to realize that he had not sufficiently thought through his previous beliefs. He began to fear that he was wasting his time on beliefs that were not true. He eventually moved away from his religious beliefs and ultimately embraced atheism.

This story is not proof that higher education automatically deprives religious believers of their faith. The high number of religious individuals with college degrees provides evidence that individuals often obtain higher education without losing their faith. However, this story, and others like it from among our respondents, indicates that institutions of higher education can provide a pathway by which some individuals leave their faiths. Since institutions of higher education are seen as places where scientific research is conducted, the occurrences of individuals becoming atheists due to their college experiences reinforces the assumptions of atheists that their ideology is scientifically based. We will investigate these assumptions more deeply in later chapters where we look at the perceptions that atheists have of science, rationality, and religion.

SOME QUALITATIVE CHARACTERISTICS OF ATHEISTS

Beyond our assessment of the quantitative descriptions of atheists, we also found some useful initial qualitative patterns worth pointing out, particularly from the face-to-face interviews. For example, we found that nearly two-thirds of those we interviewed (65.2 percent) stated that they never had any doubts about their atheism. When we asked them whether they ever had doubts about their atheism, some of the interviewees expressed this lack of doubt in very strong terms.

> No, never. I know the "There are no atheists in foxholes," and that sorta theory, but I've really never been tempted to think otherwise, no. (John)

> Not at all. Never. Never. As a matter of fact, since I realized that I was an atheist, my take on atheism has only gotten stronger. (Francis)

We found this percentage to be fairly high considering that many atheists took pride in the fact that they saw themselves open to alternative possibilities. In fact, some of them critiqued religion as not being a system open to new truths, whereas atheism was based on science, a system in which new evidence brings about new answers.

> I think science is a method of study and I think religion is a desire for something to be true. Science you can approach with the assumption that something is true and set about seeing if you can prove or disprove it, but the scientific method is supposed to eliminate the falsities. Religion doesn't operate that way. Religion, you started out with the truth and everything else is going to prove why it's true. So I don't think the two are related. (Wilma)

> I guess a lot of people would say that they are both kind of concerned with knowing, but I want to say the religious—they have already made up their mind and you know they are not investigating anything. So, I just still really see relationship. Science is about findings, truth you know in general, and now it is a methodology to find truth. (Peter)

Given such a critique of religion, one would expect more individuals to discuss the possibility of doubting their conclusions about atheism. Yet even individuals who perceive themselves as objective are often vulnerable to biases that created the conclusions they have drawn. The social position of atheists can feed into a motivation for a philosophy that is not otherworldly.

Their certainty that they have the most rational approach can buttress a confidence of their worldview and meet their cultural and social desires.

It can be argued that the lack of doubt of atheists is due to the overwhelming evidence they draw on to create their conclusions about religion. Yet, surprisingly, only half of all atheists we interviewed offered positive evidence for atheism. The other half generally contended that the evidence for atheism was the lack of evidence for the supernatural. A typical statement of this kind came from Timmy: "I can't think of an oral argument for atheism besides the other lack of proof for any religion." Instead of powerful arguments for atheism, such answers reveal that atheism may be a default position for those who do not perceive sufficient evidence for the supernatural. However, atheism is generally not supported by powerful positive evidence for the belief that deities and/or the supernatural do not exist. Thus, it is surprising that individuals who perceive themselves as quite open to finding the truth wherever it may lead them have so few doubts about their current belief system. Such a propensity speaks to the possibility of atheism being less of a rational system and more of an ideology that meets important social needs for individuals who embrace this belief.

A final qualitative initial observation to make of atheists is a fairly common response they have to the influence of the writings of other atheists. When we asked the respondents if there was someone who influenced them toward accepting atheism, several of them commented that the person who influenced them did so through their writing.

> I think it was after I got divorced, about a couple of years after that, that's when I started reading a lot more. There was more prominent stuff with people like Christopher Hitchens, Richard Dawkins and stuff that were coming out, as far as in the news and the more I started reading about it, that's when I started going toward being a full-fledged atheist. (Mickey)

> And as I began reading Ayn Rand and some of the related literature, then I said, "Well, yeah, it sounds like they've got the right idea, I can understand this, and this makes sense to me." So I began to shift over to the feeling that I was really an atheist and not an agnostic. (Abraham)

In fact, atheists we interviewed stated that they were much more likely to be influenced to become an atheist by a person they did not personally know, usually the author of a book that they respected (42.2 percent of them were so influenced), than by someone who was a personal friend or family member (only 8.9 percent were so influenced). Personal contact is not highly influential for moving individuals toward atheism. This is not to say that the families and friends of atheists are unimportant. The fact that atheists are likely to grow up in families where religion is relatively unimportant indicates that social interactions do help shape the probability that someone will be an atheist. But atheists tend to trace their evolution toward atheism through reading books rather than through personal interaction.

The linking of influence to reading of books rather than interaction with others is important for the narrative many of the respondents told us. The narrative of our respondents is that atheism is a rational inevitability as opposed to the emotional irrationality of religion. We came away from the interviews convinced that there were subcultural values among atheists that promoted rationality above most other values. Such subcultural values can be reinforced through the literature produced by the atheists. For example, the value of rationality was reinforced by the primary literature written by atheists. The authors of this literature discuss how atheists' search for truth is the motivating factor for why they come to their conclusions about the supernatural, as the following excerpts from articles in the primary atheist literature indicate:

> I tried to keep quiet, even on occasion pretended to believe, but eventually it would all come unraveled. My failing was that I had too much respect for the truth.

> The only justifiable approach to find the truth and creating progress is with pure reason, as opposed to tradition, superstition and dogma.

Such statements indicate that a message atheists receive from their literature is that there is a truth out there to be found with rational thinking. For atheists, that truth is the absence of the supernatural. Some of our respondents did not understand how thinking people could believe in the supernatural. In fact, one of the articles in the primary literature was titled "Why Do Believers Avoid Facts?" The article goes on to say, "Our ethics come from society, evolutionary biology, rational discourse, and value-based decision making." Clearly this article argues that logic dictates an atheist perspective on the supernatural and on society. It is a message that our respondents have not missed. They paint a world where acceptance of atheism is the most logical conclusion a person can make. With this perception reinforced by the literature that they read, it is no surprise that we found a common value of rationality among our respondents.[14]

Even though respondents often claimed that they were not influenced by others in their acceptance of atheism, there is still a community that helps to reinforce their beliefs. Some of them commented that they desired the sort of interpersonal interactions that religious individuals gain from their churches and synagogues. But values can be communicated by literature as well as in person. Atheists tend to use the same argument that they've read in a given book or heard from a certain speaker. For example, more than once we had a respondent make favorable reference to the "teapot argument" developed by

Bertrand Russell.[15] A study of atheists is a study, among other things, of a subculture that communicates its values through literature perhaps even more than through interpersonal contact.

While there were some respondents who indicated emotional reasons for their acceptance of atheism, such respondents were the exception and not the rule. But it is quite possible that emotions played a more important role in the acceptance of atheism than the respondents let on. Individuals generally learn the values of subcultures and reinforce those values among themselves. There is little reason to believe that such reinforcement does not happen even through literature. The literature read by atheists can communicate to them the accepted values of the atheist community. The atheists themselves can engage in image management to represent those values to others. Thus, while we take our respondents at their word, we also have to be aware of their need to project the images of rationality and individual agency that the respondents may be motivated to project. For example, one of the respondents made a point of saying that she did her own research about becoming an atheist and that no one person influenced her decision. And yet she also stated, "I had just started dating somebody new, and I don't think he influenced it, but he considered himself an atheist. I had never met anybody until this point who had said, 'I'm an atheist.' I never thought that that was another possibility" (Marsha). Objectively, it is plausible to state that her boyfriend provided her with an example of atheism that she had never seen before. This means that he was an important influence in her eventual acceptance of atheism. We do not think that our respondent was lying. We contend that a reconstruction of an identity as an atheist helps her to see her decision as a purely rational one that she arrived at by herself even though there was a boyfriend who gave her the idea that atheism was possible. We point this out to note that it is important to take into consideration the need of atheists to project a rational persona and to suggest the power of this self-image of rationality.

Preliminary analysis of our data indicates that atheists perceive themselves as more rational than other individuals in society. This perception of rationality empowers atheists subscribe to the idea that they have found a transcendent truth about the absence of supernatural reality. Whether this confidence is derived from successes in other areas of life or whether their confidence about their atheism motivates them to take responsibility for themselves and thus contributes to their economic/educational triumphs cannot be determined from this study. But there is no denying the confidence atheists have in their thinking about the supernatural. We will show in chapter 5 that this confidence also extends to their understanding of our society and their political orientation. But for now it is useful to look at the nature of this confidence in general. Given the fact that atheism is ultimately unprovable, a fact that our respondents recognize, why do such highly educated individuals speak with such confidence about adopting this epistemological system of thought? We need to more fully explore the extent and source of the confidence that so many of our respondents exuded. In the next chapter we will do just that as we look at our respondents' arguments about the irrationality of religion and how this illogical belief system creates problems in our society.

Chapter Four

The Foolishness of Religion

Particularism, in the context of religion, is the notion that one's particular religious belief is correct and all others are wrong. An image that comes from this type of particularism is the evangelical Christian who believes that he or she must convince others of the rightness of his or her belief and that his or her deity is the right one. Those who do not accept the "right" path to that deity are seen as doomed for eternal punishment. This type of particularism is connected to the propensity of such individuals to proselytize, a feature that several atheists in our online sample expressed disdain for. We did not see a lot of the type of proselytizing among atheists that evangelical Christians are known for. However, we did pick up on notions of particularism in that atheists tend to be convinced that supernaturalism is a myth and all religious beliefs are incorrect. Even as many of them admit that they cannot prove that atheism is the only correct belief, they contend that the evidence is that there is no deity and it is foolish to believe otherwise.

In this chapter we will more fully explore the confidence atheists have in their beliefs about the supernatural. We will see how they construct their arguments about the illogical nature of religion. From that point we will be in a position to see how this confidence in their atheism impacts their perception of religious individuals. Noting the low consideration they have for the cognitive abilities of those individuals will help us to understand their comprehensive view of society and their place in society.

THE IRRATIONALITY OF RELIGION

Earlier work of ours established that cultural progressives tend to think of cultural conservatives as irrational.[1] Part of that irrationality is the reliance of such individuals on otherworldly entities for support and guidance. The atheists in our online survey and those we interviewed also confirmed the idea of irrationality as they critiqued religious belief. As we established in the last chapter, atheists do not tend to rely upon positive arguments for atheism. Rather, they tend to point out what they perceive as the illogical thinking of people of faith.

> The Christian probably just accepted his creed through tradition, fear and conformity, which I find weak and illogical. (male, 36–45, master's degree)

> With the dogmatic ideology, any crazy person can interpret the bible to give them support to do terrible things. One example out of the many is the bible was used to support slavery in the south during the civil war. Today it's been used to oppress innocent minorities like racial, women, and gay equality. Accepting things without evidence, in other words, faith or dogma, encourages people to accept things irrationally, which leads to harming others. (female, 26–35, some college)

> The end result is that if there's a God, it either does not get involved or if it gets involved, it's in a way that nobody can see, nobody can prove. Okay, there is no floating heads that float over cities that everybody sees. Okay, there's no huge miracles that are viewable and seeable and doable. So basically, if God doesn't get involved, or if he does it so sneakily that nobody knows, to the average person, the average day, it's exactly like no God exists. Now again, does he exist or not? It doesn't matter. It doesn't matter because the average person can't deal with it. (Nick)

> It was always easy to dismiss people like Jerry Falwell (gays caused hurricane Katrina, 9/11, etc.), Pat Robertson (another hurricane moved away because of his prayers) as nut jobs despite the fact they are considered influential. Here is someone in my home town, electing leader—no—actively working against people of different religious ideas, or even of those who have a different idea of religion's involvement in politics. Anytime someone I would consider a member of the Christian Right gets up to speak, I immediately assume all the characteristics of that voter plus the irrationality of the "celebrities" mentioned above with that person. I have to make an effort to treat the person as an individual. (male, 46–55, bachelor's degree)

Furthermore, the primary literature buttresses the notion of irrationality among people who believe in the supernatural.

> Religious people are susceptible because they are groomed not to question and to dedicate their lives to a "higher power," a power that is utterly silent (whether or not "God" is deaf, he is without a doubt dumb).

> It is time for those who challenge religion to come out of the closet, as it were. It is time to stare religion of any stripe in the face with fierce and undaunted truth, the truth that belief in imaginary friends is natural and expected in a

6-year-old. But just as a child develops and then rejects childish ideas, so must humankind abandon belief in an omniscient, omnipotent being.

Even the terms atheists use to describe themselves, such as "free thinker" and "rationalist," denote the idea that there is a truth about supernaturalism they have found. This truth is one that others have not had the insight or ability to perceive. It is, for them, truth that all religions are false and there is no supernatural reality.

Because atheists have a tendency to see people of faith as irrational, they have a hard time understanding how individuals maintain religious beliefs. Several times respondents in our online survey indicated that they had a difficult time believing that seemingly intelligent individuals held on to illogical beliefs.

> Not too long ago learned that my aunt, an educated corporate attorney, is a young-earth creationist. I was astonished to learn that she did not require the same kind of "proof" for her religious ideology that she would require in a court of law. (female, 46–55, master's degree)

> A very good friend of mine and his wife are members of the Christian Right. He is an endodontist, she is a highly intelligent housewife—extremely bright. I vividly remember her telling me that her marriage was better because she had decided to become subordinate to her husband as mentioned in the Bible. I was incredulous, but could do nothing to change her mind. (male, 66–75, doctorate)

> Dining at a medical meeting with fellow physician, who stated that they never have "proved" evolution—"it's only a 'theory'" . . . I just shook my head and changed the subject with this scientifically educated man who chose to ignore his educational background. (male, 66–75, doctorate)

These three responses are fairly representative of the disbelief in some atheists toward seemingly smart individuals possessing religious beliefs. Several of our interviewees also expressed astonishment at the acceptance of religion by seemingly intelligent individuals. We can see this struggle in one of our interview respondents. Exploring the life of Ralph allows us to see the development of these thoughts. Ralph is an older man who had Jewish parents who largely rejected their faith. As such, he was raised "post-religion." For Ralph, what this meant was that his parents were not going to raise him in "any particular way."

> So, they really did, I do not think what they consider themselves, atheist or agnostic, they are just like, okay. This does not make sense to us, but you guys are kind of figure out later on what you want to do.

What Ralph decided to do was to become an atheist. In fact, he described himself even as a little kid as a "weak atheist." He describes this state as not believing in the supernatural but not having much of a stake in believing or not believing. In other words, although he did not believe in the supernatural, atheism did not matter much in the way he lived his life. As he went to college, his feelings hardened to the point that he began to believe that he couldn't "understand how anybody who is you know rational in this day and age could possibly be religious." Early in his life, Ralph came to the conclusion that religious belief is proof of irrationality.

Compounding Ralph's belief is the limited exposure he has had to people of faith. Ralph himself admits that he "had no exposure [to religion] which is relatively unusual because obviously most people are raised in a religious setting." Ralph did remember being in a Methodist church for his first marriage. Before that he attended two or three classes in a Presbyterian church to try to understand why people had religious faith. He concluded,

> I can't get there from here. I understand what you are saying whatever, but you know I am kind of scientific background; I was a mathematician, who has got a degree. It does not make a lot of sense; I cannot understand this and that he said well, understand that this has to be faith and I looked and I said it does not make any sense logically at all. I can't get there from here and so there is not going to be anything that I can see doing because it literally makes no sense to me, religion made no sense.

From that point on, Ralph avoided religious functions. He dismissed the possibility of religion becoming part of his life. It was not something for him to think about unless someone brought up the subject. Thus atheism was merely a natural logical consequence of his inattention to religious matters. His desire to have little to do with religion was strong enough that he told the interviewer, "If my wife suddenly decided she is having a conversion and became religious, I will file for divorce the next day." Later in the interview Ralph mentioned that, for the most part, he is not comfortable with religious people and the most he would be comfortable with are individuals who define themselves as "spiritual," although he is not sure what that means.

Now, as he heads toward the end of his life, he still wonders why religion persists. Ralph struggles to understand why scientific advances have not convinced individuals of the irrationality of religion. Ralph talked about how thinking people should lose their religious faith in high school. He was especially confused by the idea that scientists can have religion. For Ralph, science and religion do not mix, as he sees science as "based on the idea of experimentation involving knowledge and change of knowledge" while religion is "fundamentally based on faith and I don't see particularly how they (science and religion) can coexist." Accordingly, Ralph contends that for individuals to have religious beliefs, they must be ignorant of science. This makes it difficult for him to understand how a highly educated scientist is able to retain religious faith. In fact, he stated toward the end of the interview, "It would be an interesting conversation to have somebody highly intelligent, you know well-educated person that has a religious belief that might be a conversation I will undertake, it is going to be really curious to see how they can reconcile that."

Ralph truly struggles to accept the fact that an intelligent person can be religious. He likely struggles more with an inability to understand how intelligent people can be religious than other atheists, but the struggle itself is quite common among atheists. Many of them simply do not believe that a logical individual can have religious faith. For them, nonbelief is the only rational approach for an individual.

Ralph's story indicates how some atheists struggle with the possibility that religious belief is not limited to irrational individuals. This was particularly more likely to occur among the atheists we interviewed who lived in areas that were not highly religious. For such atheists, it was not uncommon for them to have a hard time conceptualizing a rational person of faith. Ralph's story also reveals another common thread among some atheists, which is that they see themselves as having been atheists from a very early age. From a very early age religion did not make sense to many of these atheists. In fact, some of our respondents contend that people are born atheists and must be socialized into having a religious belief. They sometimes see themselves as lucky to have found atheism early in their lives, although some, like Ralph, take a brief stab at learning why some people may be religious. But, like Ralph, they generally submerge themselves in their atheist beliefs at an early age and isolate themselves from religious influences.

However, not all atheists grow up without supernatural beliefs. We did find some atheists who grew up with a religious tradition. Some of them even spoke fondly of the time when they had religious beliefs. However, later these individuals lost their religious beliefs and embraced atheism. College was often a key time in which they began to challenge the assumptions surrounding their faith and to eventually leave their faith.

> When I was in college, I had what I call an epiphany. I was in an anthropology class . . . this young man, young instructor, said that all the cultures that they've been able to study in the world have had some form of afterlife. It just—I remember, it was like an electric thing went off in my body and I thought—I did not think, oh, my gosh, everybody understands what's true; what I thought was, oh, my gosh, everybody's afraid to die. It was a huge revelation to me. The fact that every culture has some form of afterlife, to me, was proof of there being no religion. So, that was very important. (Nicole)

> Well, I had taken that world religion class. That was very vital to that turning point because we kind of took apart a lot of the beliefs I had, a lot of the

questions that I still had. I had a lot of questions during that course and I kind of found out that the questions that I had were all based on the idea that religions were made from storytellers, men, ages ago. Once I put that into perspective, a lot of the stories and a lot of the things made sense to me in a way that I understood, kind of, more of the history of it and that it was made up, I guess I could say. So, that class kind of influenced my decision a lot. (Marsha)

Both of these individuals were religious at one point in their lives and now had become atheists. It is simplistic to state that a single college class reversed their religious beliefs. Other elements in their lives were contributing to the alteration of their attitudes toward religion. In the case of the first respondent, the painful death of her father had brought about questions for her, and in the case of the second respondent, her college class coincided with a romantic relationship she started with an atheist. But while there were other circumstances that influenced their acceptance of atheism, clearly the college experience also played an important role in their movement away from religious belief.

Using college experiences as a reason for leaving their religion buttresses atheists' conviction about the rationality of their beliefs. It allows for atheists to look back at their transition from religious to nonreligious as moving from emotional indoctrination to a rational appreciation of the truth. One atheist (Bill) had been converted to Christianity due to the friendships he developed with Christians. Over time he began to question the rational foundations of his faith and eventually became an atheist. He noted, "My conversion to Christianity . . . was definitely influenced by friends by people that I physically spent time with. The de-conversion was much more influenced by reading people." Thus his recollection was that conversion to Christianity was an emotional experience in which relationships with others produced satisfaction while his movement away from belief was done through reading and a more rational process. Such a way of conceptualizing his movement away from religious beliefs reinforces the notion of atheism as the logical conclusion of assessing the available data, which fits into the subcultural understanding that atheists have of religion.

The story of Sam is an excellent example of how those who at one point have religious beliefs conceptualize an understanding of their lives that supports their ideas about atheism and faith. Sam grew up in a Baptist household but one that was not overly restrictive because of religion. Sam's childhood friends tended to be Christians as well. Many of those friends attended Christian schools, but his father was an educator, which influenced him to keep Sam in public schools. But Sam never felt that his religion was threatened by the public schools. He attributes this to the fact that most of the kids in his school were Christians: "I would say when I was in high school, 99.9 percent of the kids that I was in school with were Christians. In fact, the most popular kids in high school were Christians, and were socially active Christians." Growing up in a heavily Christian area of the country served to insulate Sam from non-Christian influences.

Due to this lack of non-Christian influence, Sam did not seriously question his faith as a child and adolescent.

> Honestly, I never thought about religion. I mean, I never contemplated it. These truths, as I understood them—these were instructions that were given to me by my parents! When you're a child, you trust your parents implicitly with just about everything they tell you until you become a teenager. But even then—even when I was a teenager, I didn't think to question them. It was only later when I was in college that it even dawned on me that I could question it. To me it was just such a—just an assumed reality. Why would my parents— my father was a very smart man. My mom, she's no dummy. They would not deceive me knowingly. It never occurred to me that the religion that we had could not be true.

In college Sam took a class on the Bible as literature. The class influenced him toward reading the Bible in a new way. Whereas before he accepted the general argument for the Bible, now he learned higher criticism[2] and other educational theories that challenged his traditional understanding of scripture. As he began to accept these criticisms, he began to ask himself another critical question: "Now wait a minute, if I had not been raised to accept this book as the word of God, would I?"

This questioning started him on a search for a religious fit for himself. He tried Roman Catholicism, but the sex scandals and disparities in Catholic theology led him away from it. Then he heard of a Baptist church that sponsored a question-and-answer session with three atheists. Attending it exposed Sam to Christian apologetics, or rational arguments for Christian faith. This intrigued him and the event lead to an interesting turn in his life.

> I introduced myself to both the atheists and the Christians. I thought they were both really great groups, and so I actually started attending the Sunday school class, and then I started also attending the atheist group. So the atheist group met on the first Sunday of the month. So the first Sunday of the month, I was with the atheists. The other Sundays, I was with Christians. It was fascinating. It was very fascinating to be with both sides, particularly because I became aware of how deep these, I guess, stereotypes were on both sides. So you're with the Christians, and they're like, oh, those awful atheists. And then you're with the atheists, and they're like, oh, those stupid Christians. The atheists really aren't that awful, and the Christians aren't that stupid.

But eventually the church hired a very conservative pastor who did not see the need for the innovative Sunday school group. With the end of that group, Sam only attended the atheist group, which cemented his atheist beliefs and lifestyle. He even became a leader in the group, although that leadership turned turbulent at times and eventually he left the organization, but not before solidifying his atheism. The transformation was not inevitable. Even Sam recognizes that possibility: "Sometimes I wonder what my life—if I would have stayed a Christian—if I would have gotten into apologetics . . . they [smart Christians] sort of hang their hats on, it [apologetics] sort of allows them to still be Christians. So it may have done the same thing for me. I don't know." But that did not happen and Sam had further developed his atheism over the past several years.

Sam has more respect for religious individuals than many of the other atheists in this study. His acknowledgment that Christians can be "smart" goes further than many of his atheists peers are willing to go. However, he still sees his journey as a process by which he gained intellectual enlighten-ment as he moved further away from his religious moorings. In this way he reinforces the notion of atheism of being the logical outcome of rational thinking.

Sam's story provides certain lessons about the perspectives of atheists who come out of a religious setting. Unlike atheists who have been "born atheist," these individuals are less likely to see themselves as having thought seriously about religious issues at an early age. They tend to see themselves as having undergone some awakening that allows them to put religion in the proper perspective. However, generally there are more than mere rational assessments occurring with atheists. Like Sam, there is generally an emotion-al or relational issue at play when they make their final break toward atheism or when they first start questioning their religion. For Sam, this occurred as he broke toward atheism when his church class was cancelled and he was left with only his atheist network. Ironically, the church brought Sam into contact with the atheist organization through their question-and-answer event and then led Sam into a deeper relationship with the organization by ending the class. As it concerns Sam's life, the church's actions undoubtedly created a different result from what they had originally intended with their event and cancellation of the class.

Sam retained some degree of respect for his former Christian friends. This does not always happen with atheists who leave their former religious roots. Some of the respondents were quite resentful of having being misled for so many years. Both atheists who have been nonbelievers since being young children and those who were "deconverted" to atheism later in their lives have animosity toward people of faith. But it is possible that those who later become atheists have a stronger level of anger since they can be more likely to feel deprived at having been kept from what is, for them, an undeniable truth.

The lack of respect many atheists possess inhibits the ability of atheists to have meaningful interpersonal relationships with religious individuals. But it also has important connotations for the role atheists perceive religious others to have in our society. Atheists are deeply concerned that these individuals for whom they have so little respect are using inferior cognitive abilities to make our society worse.

THE ABSENCE OF SCIENCE

As we have argued, atheists perceive that there is a truth that can be obtained through logical assessment of reality. This means that religion has to be the result of irrationality and faulty thinking. But atheists also bring the idea of science into their equation of religion and rationality. More specifically, atheists tend to see people of faith as individuals who are devoid of scientific learning and training. This allows them to state that those who do not accept the rational and scientific reality of atheism are illogical.

In the last chapter we pointed out that many atheists contrast science and religion. These atheists perceive atheism as akin to science and science as incompatible with religion. As a result of this perception, some atheists have a dichotomous understanding in which science and religion are polar opposites. They perceive their stance supporting atheism as support of the rational application of science. For this reason, they argue that atheism is the accurate assessment of truth or reality while religion is the assertion of fantasy.

The idea of using science as the opposite of religion was a common theme for our online and interview respondents.

> I am atheist, environmentalist, support . . . science-based sex education in schools . . . I accept evolution as a proven fact that should be taught in science classes to our children. I could go on and on. The Christian Right is opposed to all this! (male, over 75, master's degree)

> Science is about finding the best way of doing things, the best knowledge that we can acquire. Religion has nothing to do with either of those, absolutely nothing. They're not compatible 'cause they're going to ignore the facts. You can't be a scientist. If you wanna be a scientist you can't be religious. They don't fit together. Oil and water. (Sam)

> The Christians . . . support myth and superstition instead of reason and science. (female, 46–55, bachelor's degree)

As a result of the perceived unwillingness of religious people to rely on science, several atheists questioned the ability of religious people to learn about truth that they are comfortable with. For the atheists, science is seen as the way to reality. Since they tend to envision a dichotomous science or religion reality, they perceive heavily religious individuals to be just as heavily anti-science. In fact, the atheists in our online survey used the term "anti-science" seventy-eight times as a way to describe the Christian Right.

Atheists have created a relatively simple calculus for their understanding of religious individuals. For them, science is the best, or perhaps the only,[3] way to understand reality. They are not nihilists, as they believe that there is a truth to be understood. Those who adhere to religious beliefs are neglecting the use of science to gain a truthful understanding of reality. As such, religious individuals cannot be counted on to find truth. One atheist whom we interviewed put this quite well with an example from a friend:

> For some people, they may not be willing to question things or are happy where they're at. I know someone who's very, very strongly a Christian, mostly because she has found happiness in religion, so to her, why upset that? Because she doesn't feel that truth has its own intrinsic value. She feels that the search for happiness has its own intrinsic value, and so it has a lot to do with your values, your personality, of course your upbringing and how you've been taught to question things and think about things. (Elaine)

Individuals often define themselves by what they are not as much as by what they are. Atheists clearly define themselves as not religious, and since they do not see themselves as religious, they perceive themselves as not having the problems they see in religion, such as the inability of the religious to use science to understand truth. Atheists perceive the opposite about non-religious individuals and especially about atheists. For many of them, being an atheist is akin to being a lover of science and truth. They contend that because atheists rely on science, they are not blinded to the truth that is out there. This sentiment is captured well in the following statement from one of our interviewed atheists:

> What an atheist is? I would say that a person that is an atheist is someone that has an objective mind. Someone that doesn't take any statement as truth. You can't necessarily say a statement is true without actually having proof, there's proof. (Francis)

Thus atheists have an important conceptual framework by which to understand religion. Religion is the abdication of seeking out the truth. Atheism is conceptualized as the courageous willingness to seek out truth through science. The particularism of atheists is built on the notion that they have used logic to determine what is true and what is not. They are convinced that the evidence they have is more powerful than any evidence religious individuals can generate since their evidence is based on science and logic while religious individuals rely on myth and superstition for their evidence. This helps them to be comfortable with the idea that atheism is an accurate assessment of reality even though it cannot be proven if the same rigorous assessment that atheists apply to religious belief systems is applied to beliefs about atheism.

This sort of dichotomous science or religion ideology can be seen in the statements of Judy. She was raised in a Methodist home by parents who had high educational expectations of her. Although Judy's parents were not very religious, many of her high school friends were and she became somewhat religious. However, she saw that some of her Christian friends did not live out the sexual expectations inherited in their religious beliefs. Furthermore, when she went off to college she began to hang around social networks that were not religious, and she did not attend religious services as often as she did in high school. Her own sexual activity began to make it hard for her to retain her religious direction. She describes what she was going through this way: "I had a big disconnect. It really caused me a lot of problems. It caused me a lot of grief because I felt very much like I was doing a lot of soul-searching in college."

Judy decided that she did not have to attend church to be a believer. As she moved away from a religious lifestyle, she began to do more reading and eventually became an agnostic. However, marriage and the birth of her child convinced her to move from being "on the fence," as she wanted to counter some of the troubling "religious" things she was hearing from her daughter. Her fear of her daughter becoming indoctrinated led her to make a stronger proclamation about her atheism.

Judy's path to atheism was driven by the inconsistency she saw in Christians, her own inconsistency with Christian sexual morality, and the writings of several atheist authors. As she describes her atheism, however, it is the latter influence that she emphasizes. Doing so allows for the claim of atheism being a rational response to the illogicality of religion. This has allowed her to contrast the rationality of atheism with the foolishness of religion. For example, as she describes her rationale to be more open about her atheism to protect her daughter, she states, "I feel better about this because I feel like it sets her up to be more critical intellectually and be more self-loving as opposed to loathing like I was growing up, you know? So, I'm hoping that that's gonna be a good influence on her." In this we see that she characterizes her atheist beliefs as not merely more rational than religious beliefs but also healthier. This indicates how she has conceptualized a dichotomous philosophical reality whereby most, if not all, positive qualities can be attributed to atheism while most, if not all, negative qualities can be attributed to religious belief.

Judy goes beyond merely seeing religion as illogical to seeing it as dysfunctional. This is because she sees logic, rationality, and science as the ways in which we can find a true path to a better life and society. She did not directly mention science in describing her move toward atheism. Unlike some of the other respondents who became atheists in college, she did not

attribute her move to some insight she had in college. However, when she is
asked later about religion and science, we once again begin to see the dichotomous philosophical perspective she brings to such questions.

> I think that science, at its core, asks questions and seeks—is always question-
> ing itself. It never accepts an answer as a truism. There's always—it's always
> retesting. I think religion is exactly the opposite. It really doesn't—I mean,
> they're not really seeking. It's just kinda cyclical reasoning and I think that it's
> just such a conversational stopper. You know, as soon as you say, "Well, it's
> that way because God said so," you know you can go this far, and then, God
> does something, and it makes it so. Not only is there a disconnect between
> science and religion, but can you really have a religious education? I mean,
> can you actually have a Christian education? Or if that doesn't somehow—at
> the very base, you start off with a false premise or an unprovable premise
> anyway. And then, everything else follows is gonna be flawed.

The disconnect that Judy sees between science and religion leads to a
perception regarding the problems created by religion. When she was asked
about the problems she saw created by religion, she focused quite a bit on the
possible intrusion of religion into our government. She singled out as a prime
example the interference of religion in our public education system. Even
though she sent her child to a private school, she still had great fear of how
this interference might be shaping the public education of kids in her region
of the country. Although she did not explicitly bring up science in her comments, given her comment above about our inability to have religion as part
of an educational system, it can be implied that part of her concern stems
from her perception of the incompatibility of religion and science.

So what kind of world would Judy like to see as it concerns religion?
When we asked her about that, she first talked about John Lennon's song
"Imagine" and *Star Trek*. Both the song and the television series offer images
of a world without religion. She then quickly shifted to Europe as a desirable
direction that we might want to go in.

> So, you know, in France, it's very secular. I wouldn't, by any means, say that
> we should all be French—by any means—but, you know, there is definitely
> much more of a separation now about these things, and people tend to be a lot
> more intellectually critical. I certainly would like to see a world that had room
> and tolerance for a lot of different beliefs and different types of people.

It is interesting to note the way in which Judy links separation of religion and
government to the idea of being more intellectually critical. It is yet another
method she uses to exhibit her propensity to articulate a dichotomous ideology whereby there is a separation of positive intellectual rationality and illogical religion that can corrupt the logic needed for good governance. Making
clear her desire for minimizing the effects of religion, she ended the inter-

view by mentioning that she once thought that Dawkins in his book *The God Delusion* was a bit heavy-handed, but she implied that now she felt his ideas might be appropriate, as she was disturbed by some of the social and political events around her.

Judy shows us the life of an atheist who is becoming more concerned about the influence of religion. From early in her life, religion did not work because it did not make sense to her sexually. She also saw religion producing wrong ideas for her daughter. As a result, it was easy for her to conceive of religion as illogical and dysfunctional while seeing atheism as a positive, rational force in society. Her conception of religion as illogical does not merely mean that she believes that religious individuals are mistaken. She also perceives them as harmful to our larger society. This is an important implication of Judy's story, as we saw time and again in our interviews of atheists. The atheists in our sample did not see religious individuals as making illogical, harmless mistakes and harming only themselves; they saw them as making illogical choices dangerous to the entire society. Dealing with the implications of the distinction atheists make between harmless but wrong and harmful choices helps us to better understand their ideas about social and political reality.

FROM TROUBLED PEOPLE TO TROUBLED SOCIETY

Atheists conceptualize religious individuals as those who have built their lives on flawed premises about the supernatural. Some respondents commented that because of this flawed premise, religious individuals suffer needlessly from guilt and sexual repression. However, most of the respondents contended that individuals have a right to hold on to these inaccurate presuppositions as long as they do not interfere with the rights of others or in the operation of government. But this tolerance ends when atheists perceive religious individuals as influencing our government and the rest of society through that government, since they believe religious individuals are irrational and are leading our society down the wrong path.

The dichotomous nature by which our respondents place notions of rationality and religion results in a desire on their part for a rational ordering of society. Their interpretation of religion as the opposite of rationality generates within them a distrust of social structures legitimated by religious principles. Thus, they perceive as a result of the irrationality of religion the creation of rules and social structures inhibiting our society from heading in the right direction. This was a theme in both the online survey and interviews of atheists.

> They [the Christian Right] seriously inhibit free thinking and intellectual advancement and promote war and a single belief system. Because they appar-

ently have more children than other members of the general U.S. population, they have too much of an influence on future generations. (male, 56–65, some graduate school)

I also think that the intertwining of religion and politics that our country has had since the late seventies, early eighties is, long term, a bad thing for the country. It's one thing for people to use their beliefs and ethics to inform them in their decisions, but many, many people in this country have gone a step or two beyond that, and seem to be insisting that their religious beliefs—I don't wanna say illegally be given preference—but just a step or two short of that. In the long run, that's not a good thing for the country. It's not what our country was—not the ideal our country was founded upon. (Richard)

Trying to interject their religious beliefs in public schools, politics, society. . . . They are worse part of America, and as long as they have influence over politics, society we cannot progress as a country/people. We will only regress, as we have for the past twenty years or so. (male, 46–55, some college)

For the atheists in these samples, religion makes society worse. While some of them acknowledge that there may be some beneficial outcomes for certain individuals due to their religious faith, generally they believe that even this positive benefit is outweighed by the negative consequences to the larger society.

For atheists, it is not merely that they disagree with people of faith; they also contend that such individuals have an illogical premise for their beliefs. Atheists are troubled that religious individuals take this illogical premise into the shaping of society. Furthermore, atheists are concerned about the ability of religious individuals to continue to propagate these illogical beliefs. By and large the atheists in the online survey contended that this indoctrination led to individuals maintaining their religious beliefs, and that without such indoctrination religion could eventually disappear. As one respondent stated, "I think that we should restrict the indoctrination of children in religious dogma and ritual. . . . The religious freedom of children is being subverted by the only device that maintains the viability of faith-based ignorance" (male, 45–56, master's degree).

Some of our interview respondents also talked about the role of socialization in the creation of a religious individual. For example, one of them told the interviewer, "I mean, people are raised in certain religions and I think it's a very hard thing to break away from or really free yourself from when you're raised that way. It becomes integral definition of—part of the definition of who you are" (Barbara). Thus, atheists tend to see religion as self-perpetuating due to the ability of people of faith to continue to create new generations of adherents by indoctrinating them at a young age. These can be seen as the followers who will eventually support more of the illogical policies that many of these atheists fear.

Ultimately, atheists have developed a particularism not premised on making sure that everyone finds the right deity but rather making sure that everyone uses rationality to come to the same conclusion. That conclusion is the irrationality of religion and the need to minimize, if not eliminate, the effects of religion in society. Those who do not subscribe to this belief are seen either as irrational themselves or as having been misled by malevolent social forces or evil religious individuals. While most atheists do not want to directly disallow religion, our respondents were not shy in stating that they want religion discouraged or drowned in a sea of rational beliefs. The combination of supporting irrational beliefs that buttress backward, or irrational, social structures and the ability of religion to self-perpetuate itself through socialization, or indoctrination, generated in the minds of some of the respondents fear about the intrusion of irrational religion into what they perceived as a potentially rational society.

Atheists have made a connection between irrational individuals and dysfunctional social structures that harm most individuals in society. However, there are alternative ways to understand the relationship between social structures and individuals.[4] The fears of the atheists become operational because of the political framework in which they tend to operate. Even though we did not directly ask either our online survey respondents or our interviewees about their political preference, the vast majority of them clearly indicated an adherence to a politically progressive philosophy that emphasizes the importance of social structure. While it has been established that political ideology can be embedded within the particular religious philosophy of a group, the results from this work also suggest that political ideology can play a role in how atheism operates in a given culture. As such, it is important to take a deeper look into how political progressivism interplays with the religious beliefs of atheists, and that is the direction we will take in the next chapter.

Chapter Five

Progressive Politics as a Tenet of Atheism

Atheists believe that they are accurate about supernatural issues. They contend that nonmaterialistic beliefs are foolish, given the contemporary scientific evidence available to us. They also believe themselves to be correct about our society's political and social realities. Just as they argue that their ability to appreciate logic allows them to have an objective perception of the supernatural, they also contend that their rationality determines the best political path for our society. In this sense atheists are not different from other religious groups with high levels of particularism in that they do not limit that particularism to understandings about the supernatural, but also make assertions about materialist reality with a high degree of certainty.

The subject of atheism does not naturally lead to a discussion of progressive politics any more than the subject of theism naturally leads to a discussion of conservative politics. Yet it has been well established that traditional religiosity in the United States is correlated to political conservatism.[1] Sometimes the linking of religion and political conservatism is overemphasized, as there are many highly politically progressive religious individuals. For example, there is clearly a linking of religiosity and the acceptance of political progressive ideology in the African American community.[2] However, the relationship of traditional religiosity and political conservatism is well established, indicating that there are at least some elements within traditional religiosity that comport with politically conservative ideals.

Since previous research has established significant links between religious beliefs and political conservatism, it is not a surprise to find that progressive political ideology is also linked to atheistic beliefs. The power of that political ideology is more than we anticipated before engaging in this project. It was not what we were looking for, and as we discovered the depth of the political entanglement of our respondents, we realized that political progressiveness is a major component of atheism in the United States. Given the theoretical desire of atheists to refute the dominant religion of the day, we should not have been surprised to find a progressive counterweight to the conservatism in traditional religion. The passion atheists possessed was often seen in the question concerning what they disliked most about religion. Many respondents started off with a list of progressive political concerns. At times we felt compelled to ask them if there were nonpolitical aspects of religion they disliked. While the respondents could always articulate nonpolitical shortcomings of religion, the fact that about half of our interview respondents brought up political issues without being prompted indicated an overriding political dynamic embedded within their atheism. While our data cannot determine whether progressive ideology precedes atheism or vice versa, exploring the nature of this link is vital to understanding atheism in the United States.

It is theoretically possible to have an atheist philosophy and also a conservative or libertarian political perspective. Yet the vast majority of our atheists exhibited a progressive political belief system. Only a couple of the respondents from our online survey indicated that they were political conservatives, and such individuals openly acknowledged that they were in the minority. This was clearly stated by one respondent when she said, "I'm an odd duck! . . . an Atheist Conservative" (female, 56–65, bachelor's degree). Among our interviewees, none of them indicated any support for political conservatism. While we did not directly ask our respondents and interviewees about their political preference, the issues that they often brought up—support for abortion and same-sex marriage, mistrust of capitalism and the military, opposition to the death penalty, support for gun control, support for increased government regulation, and support of stem cell research—clearly revealed their support for political progressive causes. Active atheism in the United States is married to political progressiveness.

Some of the respondents were very overt regarding the importance of politics to their atheism, such as this interview respondent: "I'm very passionate about the subject of atheism as I am about politics too. I mean, today it's very connected" (Tom). Since we did not anticipate how significant this political progressiveness would be among our respondents, we did not approach the question of whether political ideology led to their atheism or whether their atheism motivated their political ideology. Such a question is an important one that will, we hope, be addressed in future research. However, for some atheists political progressive ideology is so deeply intertwined with their atheism that it may be impossible to separate the two. The strength of the relationship between political progressive and atheist beliefs is too strong to happen by chance. To understand atheism, we have to explore the role political progressive beliefs play in the development and maintenance of atheists' beliefs.

THE INTERTWINING OF ATHEISM AND POLITICAL PROGRESSIVENESS

It is oversimplistic to suggest that the major dividing issue between political conservatives and political liberals is the role government plays. However, clearly the political direction of political conservatives is toward either a shrinking of, or at least a slower growth in, government while the direction of political liberals tends toward a more expansive government. Smaller government means fewer regulations and less direct control of human affairs by the dominant institutions in charge of our society and economy. It may be easier to risk not relying upon the government for efficiency, fairness, and justice if one adheres to a faith that seeks such qualities outside of the human realm. But since atheists, by definition, have no such faith, it is "rational" for them to seek any redress through a more powerful and robust government. Such a sentiment clearly places them in a more progressive political framework.

However, there are clearly a few areas where atheists do not want to see government interference. None of the atheists we interviewed or surveyed strongly supported a pro-life position or resisted a societal move toward same-sex marriage. What have been conceptualized as "social issues" in the United States reverse the role of government in the political progressive/ conservative ideology, with progressives wanting less government intrusion and conservatives wanting more. We recognize that this indicates an inconsistent political philosophy on the part of both conservatives and progressives, but such inconsistency is part of the social construction of political ideology in the United States. This inconsistency may partly be explained by the philosophical nature of atheism. While government is important in dealing with larger economic and environmental issues beyond the control of individuals, atheists seek freedom for individuals to make personal choices in their own lives. Furthermore, in the United States, Christianity's link to conservative politics is heavily influenced by moralistic ties to social issues. Atheists do not accept a morality imposed on them by a deity but rather idealize the notion that humans, once they have freed themselves from supernaturalist beliefs, can make rational choices about their own sexualities and families. In this way atheism comports with inconsistency regarding the role of the government in political progressive ideology.

The role of the government is not the only salient political issue. But research indicates that political identity becomes an important way by which many individuals perceive themselves.[3] Once individuals have accepted a given political identity, it becomes easy for them to adhere to all the notions of that philosophy. If atheists are drawn to linking their atheism with a political progressive ideology, then there will be a natural process by which they begin to adhere to all the political positions of that ideology. Thus an atheist who heads toward political liberalism out of a desire for a larger, more rational government or for the freedom to set up his or her own sexuality creates a political identity that informs the atheist about issues as diverse as the Palestinian and Israeli conflict, the death penalty, school choice, the rights of unions, gun control, and so forth. The mixing of atheism and political progressiveness can create political individuals who are just as loyal to their political philosophy and can be just as single-minded about pursuing their political goals as religious individuals can be toward the pursuit of political conservatism.

To completely understand the draw of atheists to political progressiveness, we should also consider their concern about their image of morality. Many of the atheists interviewed expressed the notion that atheists are just as moral as people of faith, or even more so. For example, one respondent stated, "So there's not necessarily a correlation between degree of belief in a supreme being and leading an ethical, moral life" (Ben). This was not limited to the responses from our interviewees. The morality of atheists came up among our online respondents as well. One typical response was "Despite being 'out of the atheist closet' all along, there are people who insist on praying for me, there are people who are astounded that I live a happy and fulfilled life and there are people who are convinced that I must have no morals" (female, 56–65, some college). Even the primary literature deals with the notion that atheists are as, or more, moral than believers. In one of the newsletters, the statement is "I feel I am a much better citizen of my community and world and family because I no longer believe in god. I make decisions on my own . . . in general I do less harm, I am more compassionate, I use actions instead of intentions (or prayers), and I am generally tougher and more resilient without god in my life." Such a concern about the morality of atheists speaks to the likelihood that they often encounter claims that they lack morality. With such pressure, it is natural for them to argue that atheism does not lead to immorality and, in fact, given the particularism among atheists, atheists likely desire to show that they have a higher level of morality than religious individuals.

A progressive political philosophy can serve as the underpinning of this assertion about atheist morality. It provides atheists with a system of morality distinguished from morality based upon traditional religion. Traditional religious morality is generally conceived of as adherence to the dictates and laws provided by a transcendent source. Atheists believe that loyalty to such a source is foolish and irrational. They argue that it is more moral for humans to take matters into their own hands with a political philosophy that directly corrects societal problems. Political progressiveness allows them to make an assertion of a superior moral system. Atheist philosophy links itself to the need to create the right social structures, allowing humans to reach their highest potential. Reliance on rationality, rather than on superstition, is seen as the best way to construct those social structures. Given this potential ideal, there is little wonder that some atheists in our interviews and the online survey freely talked about how society would be better if run by rational rather than religious and superstitious individuals.

> The perfect world for me would be you wouldn't have the religion. Everything would be based on evidence and science and people would treat each other well regardless of it. (Mickey)

> In general I want the government to be neutral in regards to religion, and that is what I fight for. I would hope that conversation and being an example of non-Christian but a good citizen and promoting education and rational thinking will help elevate the country. (male, 36–45, some college)

> And so I would prefer our government to be more—strictly secular. I feel a lot of times it crosses that bridge. And I wish it wouldn't. I would hope that in most societies, that religion wouldn't have power over everybody. That is not so required. (Jan)

We have conceptualized philosophical reasons why atheists can be tied to political progressive ideology. Indeed, previous research has provided quantitative evidence that atheists are more likely to be politically progressive.[4] How this intertwining may happen in the lives of atheists is an issue that has not been fully examined. It is useful to explore the lives of our interview respondents to gain a deeper understanding of the relationship of atheism and powerful support for political progressiveness.

POLITICAL PROGRESSIVENESS IN THE LIVES OF ATHEISTS

It is not sufficient merely to acknowledge that atheists are more politically progressive than religious individuals. In our respondents, political progressiveness was part of their atheism. It was hard to disentangle their political philosophy from their atheist beliefs. An example of this entanglement can be seen in the life of Tom.

Tom's father was a translator, which allowed Tom at a young age to travel all over Europe. After his parents divorced he found himself living in Switzerland until his late twenties. He then lived in San Francisco until his forties. Now Tom lives in an area of the country known for not being religious. Furthermore, his parents were nonreligious Jews who did not expose him to religion. Religion did not come up with his friends. It is safe to say that Tom had very little exposure to religious individuals in his upbringing and life. He did not relate witnessing any dysfunctions among religious individuals that drove him to atheism. For Tom, atheism was a highly likely consequence of his lack of contact with people of faith. As Tom himself puts it, "I could never believe because it wasn't . . . ever forced on me."

Despite the minimal amount of religious influence in his upbringing, the strong identity of an atheist was not a foregone conclusion for Tom. He saw his acceptance of atheism developing in two distinct steps. The first was merely the fact that he was not socialized to be religious and so he did not seriously consider religion a viable belief system. He did not necessarily hate religion; it just was not a part of his life. However, the second step led him to a strident anti-religion attitude. He discusses how political awareness began to shape a stronger atheist identity:

> I didn't become more philosophical and political until I was in my late teens, going to college, getting exposed to other ideas. But I think something that clearly helped push me toward being not just an atheist because I'm not interested in religion, but also an atheist to make a statement.

At this point in the interview, it was unclear what he meant about how philosophical and political ideas begin to shape his atheism or what sort of statement Tom wanted to make. Fortunately, he went on later in the interview to clarify what he meant.

> Well, when I say politics, I mean it in the most broadest sense of the word . . . I think of it in terms of how we manage power, which drives who gets what, when and where? How we distribute power and who gets power. Exactly, that's what I mean by politics. . . . So anyway, the biggest problem and concern I have with organized religion is I see it as a means to control the masses by the pew. That would be my thesis statement, and I could go on for hours talking about that. But that's kind of—that's the difference between me being an atheist just because I can't believe in these concepts, and then the other part of me being an atheist and wanting to support being a member of [name of atheist organization].

Tom's political ideals spill over into his religious philosophy. He is concerned with the power dynamics in our society and envisions religion as a dysfunctional institution because it distorts what should be a healthy distribution of power, opining that religion socializes individuals into nonbeneficial actions. Clearly Tom intertwines his political philosophy and his atheist underpinnings.

We did not have direct questions on politics, but Tom brought politics into the discussion. Tom's political philosophy is based on the notion that humans are evolving. He is focused on cultural evolution rather than biological evolution, as he states, "The evolution that we witnessed from the Renaissance to today is amazing. But there's so much more evolving that we need to do." For Tom, the impediment to this evolution is religion. He fears that religion socializes individuals into a tribal mindset that inhibits the ability of humans to fulfill societal potential. One example he gives of how religion inhibits us is belief in the Rapture and/or the belief that people are going to heaven. Because of this belief, he argues, religious people often believe that they "don't need to be concerned about all these problems that are facing us economically, environmentally." Tom contends that religion convinces people to take their eyes off our contemporary problems and makes the world worse for all of us. Tom's discussion of political issues animates him to buttress his credentials as a political progressive. He speaks of disdain for the war in Iraq. He is distrustful of conservative actions on the part of the Israeli government. He is concerned with a lack of teaching evolution in our schools. When he discusses each of these issues, he makes comments about how religious individuals tend to oppose his political positions. Religion resists what he sees as rational progress to a better society and feeds his desire to build on his strong identity as an atheist.

But beyond specific issues, Tom struggles with what he sees as an important essence of religion. It gets back to his definition of politics as who has power and the ability of religion to control others. He comments late in the interview, "I mean, proselytizing, the power of how organized religion controls people. That is also how organized religion stands in the way of progress too." This leads Tom to identify an important tendency that can emerge from religion, which is its support for totalitarian societies. He states, "Just focusing on totalitarianism, I think religion plays a big part in that danger and what we're talking about is the decisive nature of religion." Tom goes on to discuss his fears that the three major religions—Christianity, Islam, and Judaism—operate in such a way in the Middle East that their struggle for power may ignite another world war. The religionists' need for totalitarian power and domination of others is a critical concern for him, as he fears religion will lead to massive bloodshed and even the possible extinction of humans. While he did not outline political solutions to this situation, it is clear that he thinks religion plays an important role in perpetuating Middle East violence and exacerbates other political problems.

We went into depth with Tom to illustrate how atheism and political progressive philosophy often reinforce one another. At times in our interview with Tom it was difficult to tell when one began and the other one ended. Tom was not an anomaly. In many ways he was more articulate with the intertwining of his political philosophy and religious beliefs than other atheists, but we observed this relationship quite often in many of our other interviewees. Their atheism was motivated to no small degree by their desire to initiate certain political changes. This is not to say that they saw political desires as the driving force for why they became atheists. This may have been the case for some of our respondents, but most of them contended that their atheism was rationally based. However, despite these assertions of pure logic in the development of their atheist beliefs, it is clear that political concerns weighed heavily among many of our respondents. Those progressive political concerns likely factored into their acceptance of atheism and clearly matter in their desire to change our society.

This desire to promote political progressiveness motivates atheists to do more than sit back and be atheists. In fact, some of our interview respondents indicated an initial hesitation to be labeled as an atheist when they first decided that they did not believe in the supernatural. However, often it was a political issue that motivated them to accept the label of being an atheist and to become more involved. An example of such a situation can be seen in Jimmy. He developed a distrust of authority figures, and thus religion, at a very early age. But he was not an atheist at that point. As for religious individuals, he merely thought, "Well, that's your problem." However, his opinion changed with September 11, 2001. Jimmy stated that it

> galvanized political and religious opinions in North America in my opinion. And because of that it was no longer possible for me to sit on the fence. And when I saw the reactions of the religious and the believers to nonreligious I got a clearer understanding of the situation. In fact, I began to focus on it more. And focusing on it more it becomes a social issue. You can't sit on the fence. If you sit on the fence, you're on the wrong side, either one or the other.

This led Jimmy to accept the label of atheist. And not only did he accept the label, but he also became an atheist who hates religion and sees nothing good in it at all. In his words, "There is absolutely no good in it. There is no good in it, none. None, none, none, no, no, no, no good at all." His animosity was not limited to spiritual beliefs but also reflected his political attitudes. He was concerned with political activity that "would blur the lines between religion and government." Because of this blurring, Jimmy felt that politicians would not be willing to look out for his interests. He identified policy at the school board and foreign policy linked to religious ideals as examples of misguided politics due to politicians looking out for the interests of religion instead of the interests of people like him.

The desire to protect our political process from the excesses of religion was a clear element within the atheists in this study. For example, some of our interview respondents discussed their concerns about how religion is distorting our political process and pushing issues that are not healthy for our society.

> Well, I resent religion meddling in secular life in politics for one thing. I resent the fact that they seem unable to reach a budget not because they can't agree

on money but because the Tea Party people insist on, the news media say, abortion. (Jack)

I think evangelicals have had a great deal to do with redefining liberalism so that what used to be considered liberal is now almost considered radical-terroristic-type talking. So, I do. I view them as a large part of why that's happening. (Riley)

I don't know how this would be achieved, but the politicians would have an understanding that there is no scientific basis for religion and they shouldn't be making laws that infringe on people's freedoms, their individual freedoms. I'm very strong on individual rights. (Victor)

Our online respondents also exhibited a concern about the way religious individuals are invading our political system.

I find that their attempts to force religion into both politics and classrooms is disgusting. Promoting "Christian Science" through political movements instead of providing evidence in support of their "Theories" such as Intelligent Design, Abstinence only Sex Education, and School Prayer, which have been shown through actual scientific pursuit to be false at best. (male, 18–25, some college)

There are specific characteristics of the religious right are harmful to the body politic: authoritative micro-politics (of a fascist variant), anti-intellectual attitudes, repressive sexuality, us-versus-them dichotomy and a dogmatic insistence of counterfactuals, despite all evidence in front of them. Specific policy proposals range from the ridiculous to hateful. (male, 26–35, bachelor's degree)

Furthermore, these respondents were concerned about the sort of political issues that come out of religious adherence. For example, several respondents perceived religion as influencing individuals to take political positions that are not in their own best interests and make life worse for all of us.

They want to impose their irrational concepts (dogma, theology) on other people. They let their leaders, who I think may often be corrupt, lead the members against their own best interests. (male, 66–75, doctorate)

The most negative thing, out of many negative things I could say is that they get people to vote against their own self-interests. An example of this is getting poor evangelicals to vote Republican when the party does nothing to help the poor. Or opposing universal health care, which would be in their interest. (male, 56–65, some graduate school)

Finally, it should be noted that atheists' primary literature buttresses this notion of religion intruding on legitimate political concerns. Since atheists value reading this literature, it helps to inform them of the proper values they should support.

> In fact, religion almost ALWAYS meddles in politics—it always has and it always will, because again, it can't stand alone. It needs support from the state, and over time has established such support as a standard right that religion solely enjoys—never to be debated or even considered.

> With a new fundamentalist movement growing in size and political strength, it is imperative we do not shirk our responsibilities as secular Americans. The wall between state and church is under attack, and it is our duty to fiercely protect it.

> Calling upon commissioners and citizens to rise and pray (even silently) is coercive, embarrassing and beyond the scope of secular county government.

Progressive political concerns are an important part of atheism in the United States. Since we did not make an effort to assess the potential political elements in the causality of atheism, we stop short of stating that these political concerns create atheist desires. However, they clearly are part of developing a strong atheist identity for many atheists and buttress how atheism is promoted. Future work on atheism should take into account the role progressive political attitudes play in the creation of an atheist identity. We will initiate this process by using the answers many of our respondents gave us to look deeper into the political world of atheists and gain more knowledge of how this political view supports and is supported by their atheist perspectives.

THE POLITICAL WORLD OF ATHEISM

Atheists obviously oppose the politically conservative perspectives many religious individuals possess. But merely knowing what atheists oppose is not sufficient for us to understand what political reality atheists tend to support. It has been argued that religious individuals have a more authoritarian perspective of society.[5] This perspective is based upon the argument that religious individuals are more comfortable conforming to a traditional societal norm. The atheist's desire to refute religion leads to an opposition to such conformity and more openness to societal alterations. Indeed, on many of the social issues atheists do support more nonconformity and oppose the movement of religious individuals toward imposition of traditional sexual mores, or "family values."

> I guess the sexual deal, it's like sex is such a normal human function and when you put a lot of religious stuff on it, it gets weird and it gets funny and then you

can shun people for getting pregnant and having sex and you can just do all kinds of weird stuff. (Allison)

They have a fascist agenda. They are against gay rights, and the reproductive rights of women. They are ultra-nationalistic, and support conservative "family values" but do not clearly define these values. (male, 56–65, doctorate)

[The Catholic Church] really worked with some conservative members of Congress to really restrict women's access to birth control and abortion. That was—as a fertile individual, that's really an important issue to me, and I really felt like that was just outside the Church's—I couldn't support a church— yeah, I couldn't sit there and support an organization that would take away women's ability to control something so important to their health and their economic independence. (Shirley)

I support a woman's right to choose whether or not to abort her fetus. I believe that homosexuals should enjoy the same rights as heterosexuals. I believe in evolution. By and large, Christian fundamentalists oppose these views. (male, 66–75, some graduate school)

Promoting such diversity can comport with the social positions of atheists in that they generally have more educational and economic resources than other individuals and thus more of an ability to enjoy sexual freedom. This diversity also links to the idea that in a materialist world it is the individual who makes decisions about what is best for himself or herself. There is no deity that has created rules for the individual to live by, and so rational reflection becomes the guiding force for individuals to make such decisions.

However, it is a mistake to believe that atheists are absolutist about governmental intervention. In fact, as we left the realm of sexual and family decisions, the atheists who answered our online survey were quick to argue for the importance of the government in providing resources for the poor in society.

They [the Christian Right] are anti-government, but the government is there to help ALL people. IT's every man for himself with these people, forget the poor and needy. (male, 36–45, some graduate school)

[The most negative thing about the Christian Right is] their total opposition to government programs to help the poor. (male, 66–75, master's degree)

I've seen them justify their selfishness and lack of concern for the poor by saying they give to charity and therefore their taxes shouldn't be given to the poor. But then you find out that most if not all of their giving goes to their church and only a small part of that giving goes to help the needy. So in reality without their taxes and only such a small portion going to the needy, there is really no help for the needy. (male, 36–45, bachelor's degree)

In theory, capitalism is an economic system in which individuals make rational decisions for themselves and those decisions will benefit our society. This is similar to the argument that individuals should make the best decisions for themselves as concerns family and sexuality to maximize their happiness and make this a better society. But atheists do not accept that argument regarding economic matters. Instead, they contend that a rational government intruding on the economy is what is best for society.

The idea of a large rational government controlling much of what happens in society is quite attractive to atheists if we consider their position in society. Since they are highly educated individuals and see themselves as being more rational than their religious counterparts, it is natural for them to see themselves as important governmental leaders. Having a larger government can mean more overall social power for atheists. Our social position is important in shaping our social attitudes. Private economic organizations, some of them religious in nature, are often run by entrepreneurs without the educational training of individuals in the higher social echelons of society. The success of such organizations may not greatly aid the highly educated and wealthy individuals who tend to be atheists. By supporting the value of the public sector, atheists are in a better position to gain even higher levels of social status. This incentive offers at least a partial explanation for why atheists look toward the public sector, as opposed to the private sector, to solve our economic woes.

Beyond the incentive their social position gives them as they ponder the worth of a larger public sector, atheism itself may provide some atheists justification for seeking a larger and more powerful government. It is here that the particularism of atheists comes into play. Atheists perceive themselves as rational in comparison to the irrationality they see within religious individuals. Since atheism dismisses the idea of a transcendent being, our society has to rely upon rational, intelligent individuals to gain direction. Naturally, atheists would see themselves as individuals who are in a position to determine that direction. This is one of the reasons why some of our respondents were concerned with the presence of religious individuals in governmental positions.

> They should be restricted from voicing any opinions or solutions based on, revolving around or referring to any religion. Any failure to do so should result in that individual/or group being barred from political/government activity. (female, 26–35, bachelor's degree)

> I think religion has no business either in school or in government. (Ramon)

> [I support] laws against their proselytizing and against their being in any form of government. (female, 56–65, some college)

A rational and scientifically based government is the goal of atheists. They believe such a government would generate freedom as it concerns individuals' sexual and family choices even as it provides economic and political direction for our society.

The atheists' desire to rely upon governmental intervention is tied to their orientation toward structuralism. The distinction between a free-will individualism and a social structuralist orientation within a religious community is enunciated in Emerson and Smith's analysis of white and black Protestants. They found that white Protestants tend to adopt an individualist perspective by which they argue that success is determined by the efforts of individuals. Black Protestants were more likely to have a structuralist orientation in that they argue that social structures are an important determinant for why individuals succeed. Given the history of oppressive social structures that African Americans have endured, it makes sense that African Americans see the power of social structures to affect their lives. However, European-American Protestants tend to ignore the potential of social structures to influence social outcomes and instead rely upon the notion of relationships to alter behaviors and change society. The distinction between white and black Protestants is all the more striking in that these individuals have a high agreement on theological issues but still maintain powerful differences in their perception of social structure and individuals' efficacy in society.

Atheists definitely disagree with black Protestants on theological issues, but many of our respondents showed much of the same concern for social structure exhibited by this religious group. For atheists, the way to change society is to change the social structures in that society. For example, many of our respondents exhibited concerns about how our educational institutions influence individuals in an adverse way.

> It is an indictment of our sorry educational system that produces so many people with such appalling ignorance of the truth of the origin of the earth and of our evolutionary history. What's more, the so-called Christians should have been far more concerned about careful stewardship of the land long, long ago than they have been. Even now many are so foolish as to think there's no such thing as global warming and serious problems with rising temperatures in sea water, melting glaciers, polluted air, water, and soil that affects ALL of us in one way or another. (female, 46–55, high school diploma)

> Then it's like, their religious convictions, they try to translate them into public policy, essentially, or when they want to treat creationism in the schools, they want to get rid of birth control, they want to teach abstinence-only sex education in schools, that kind of thing. That general cluster of things, that's what worries me the most. (Frank)

> However, when that religious belief starts to intrude on my life, starts to hinder public education, or threatens to turn our country down the path to a theocracy,

> I have a huge problem. The Christian Right tends (lately) to want to do just that. Whether it's teaching ID/Creationism in public schools, denying climate change, being generally anti-science. (male, 36–45, bachelor's degree)

Because of their concern with the ability of educational organizations to negatively influence individuals, atheists are especially worried about the ability of religious individuals to adversely alter our educational institutions. Typical of those concerns are the representative answers of these respondents on issues such as teaching evolution in schools, emphasizing the concept of church/state separation in history classes, allowing religious influence on school boards, and providing sex education. Religious influence in these areas is seen as problematic since these influences can alter educational social structures to perpetuate what they see as irrational religious ideology.

If there is a social structure more important to the political identity of atheists than education, it is the government. Many respondents discussed the importance of church/state separation. It was a common theme among our online respondents.

> Like cockroaches—invading our governments, schools, libraries, etc. Tearing down the wall of separation of church and state. (male, 66–75, some college)

> They should be just as free to express their opinions as I am. I would like to see their influence contained outside of politics and schools, but that is just an enforcement of the separation of church and state that we are already supposed to have. (male, 26–35, doctorate)

> I believe in the separation of church and state even though they don't. I realize that if given the chance they would legislate me out of existence while I on the other hand, recognize their constitutional right to their particular madness. (male, 56–65, some college)

And church/state separation came up often with our interview subjects.

> So there's an ideal transition and then there would be an ideal, once you've kinda killed off religion, the transition probably just needs to be where we already are in America of separation of church and state, and continual progression of scientific learning. (Alexander)

> Well, I have a number of concerns. Fortunately, we have separation of church and state but that is forever being infringed upon by people that want to put their beliefs on someone else. (Henry)

We would also be remiss not to note that this was a topic many of the organizations that cater to atheists commonly discuss. In fact, one of the ways in which they legitimate their existence is as defenders of the rights of atheists and of church/state separation in our society. For example, on the website of one group we read that they see themselves as "the premier organization laboring for the civil liberties of atheists and the total, absolute separation of government and religion." We see further evidence in one of the funding letters from another such organization, which stated that it is "building on its momentum to fight religion in government, promote acceptance of freethinkers and interject some desperately needed reason into the public debates on religion." These and other organizations serving atheists do not always directly promote progressive politics, but they do consistently promote working against the intrusion of conservative religion politics and conceptualize this as a way to promote the rights of atheists.

Separation of church and state is an important concept in the atheist political framework, but it is not always clear what is meant by church/state separation. In previous work we noticed how the phrase "separation of church and state" can have distinctive meanings among cultural progressives. For example, some use the phrase in a defensive manner so that their rights will not be violated, while others use the phrase to justify limiting the rights of religious individuals. While a diversity of meaning is also likely among atheists, it is clear that the overall meaning of church/state separation is the reduction or elimination of religious influence in government. Several of our respondents indicated their concern about the way religious individuals shape the decisions made by our government.

> Religion . . . pervaded the U.S. political arena basing legislative decisions on the premises of a book with direct disregard and contempt for empirical observation or reason. (male, 18–25, some college)

> Keep all religions out of government and vice versa; no faith based initiatives, no holy wars, no tax exemptions, no national days of prayer, no creationism taught in public schools, no political decisions based on religious beliefs. (male, 36–45, master's degree)

> Well, I guess the transition when it happened during the Bush presidency, and when you have people who think they're talking to God and they're the head of your country, it's a little scary to me, and I don't think that the dumbest guy in the room should be president. I think that the smartest guy in the room should be president. And I just don't think that kind of leadership is good in taking on faith and God is on your side, and then doing things like starting wars and those kind of things. (Timmy)

The concern of atheists is that religious individuals take over the government, and their control of social structures thereby prevents us from developing the type of society atheists desire. They see religious individuals taking over the government to produce a theocracy or even just to channel more governmental resources to religious groups. They often resent government support that they see as aiding in the success of religious institutions. The issue of tax breaks for religious organizations came up time and time again. Atheists exhibited a concern that these tax breaks gave religious organizations an unfair advantage.

> Laws could be enacted against certain behaviors or practices that unfairly favor the Christian Right. Clergy, for example, should get no special treatment, as they now do with certain tax laws. (male, 36–45, doctorate)

> I strongly believe that all churches should be taxed. They are not just religious organizations. It is impossible to separate your religious beliefs from your political beliefs emotionally or logically. The fact is that they are very involved in political issues . . . and no matter how they try to keep themselves separate from the church they are religious. Our city just saw a 25 million-plus dollar megachurch built. The land owned by that church would provide our city with approximately a quarter of a million dollars a year in taxes. The church does nothing to support anything in our city except itself. Yet the pastor can, with a simple phone call, get the principal of our high school to stop an English teacher from using any book by Dan Brown or try to influence our GSA's organizations "Day of Silence." Tax the churches. (female, 46–55, master's degree)

> Also, I want churches and religious people to pay their taxes. Even the British royal family in England now pay taxes, so the church can catch up to the twenty-first century and pay their own taxes, especially here in Texas. (Butch)

> I think they should not be allowed to deduct from their taxes the sum of the donations they make to religious organizations and that churches should not be exempt from taxation. These things are unfair and unconstitutional. (female, 46–55, doctorate)

It is true that few respondents supported what might be called oppressive measures against religious individuals, such as not allowing them to run for political office. Most respondents indicated willingness for religious individuals to have the freedom to practice their beliefs. Yet they saw religious organizations as having an unfair advantage over other businesses[6] because of the tax breaks they receive from the government. This allows atheists to conceptualize the removal of tax breaks for religious organizations as a way of leveling the playing field rather than as a way of unfairly punishing religious organizations.

Educational and governmental structures received the most attention from the respondents in our study. Their fears of a potential invasion of religion into these structures motivate many of them to promote secular, and progressive, social structures that would stop this invasion. Political activism was the commonly accepted methodology used by atheists. In keeping with their focus on structuralism, atheists did not tend to rely on interpersonal relationships in the same manner that Emerson and Smith documented for white Protestants. A few discussed trying to change the opinion of others around them, but a similar number mentioned that they would not try to persuade religious individuals to give up their beliefs. Some of the interview subjects even stated that they understood why the religious beliefs of individuals may help them to cope with life, and thus they had no desire to try to alter those beliefs.

> I think it is fine that people believe in whatever spiritual beliefs they feel are necessary to support them morally or support them in terms of what they do in times of stress. Personally I do not feel like I need that sort of help myself and so I would not create a society that outlawed that or anything like that. Obviously you know some people do find support, they find encouragement. (Dan)

> Well, honestly, religious people, I feel that they need a crutch. They don't have the willpower to do it on their self. So they feel if they believe in a higher power, that it's gonna help them get through any times in turmoil that they have to deal with. . . . But to each their own. I'm not gonna knock anybody for their religion; what religion that you are. I'm a people person. If you're a cool person and you're fun to be around, I'm gonna hang out with you regardless of what you believe in. (Orlando)

As long as religious individuals did not intrude upon the rights of atheists, some respondents were perfectly content for them to hold on to what atheists think are mistaken, foolish ideas. For atheists, there is not a consistent desire to use interpersonal relationships to alter society, but there is a much more consistent demand for political changes. Since we sought out atheists through atheist organizations and contacts with atheists in those organizations, it is possible that we tended to find those atheists who were the most outspoken and thus most likely to be political activists. However, the fact that there was not also a correspondingly strong desire among atheists to use interpersonal relationships to create social changes indicates the relative importance of social structure as opposed to interpersonal relationships among atheists.

In fact, there is evidence that atheists may not consider interpersonal relationships to be a proper venue for contesting religious ideas. Many of the atheists were upset by efforts to proselytize them.

> Political opinions are just opinions. Being conservative doesn't make a person right or wrong. Also, people don't proselytize their political points of view. Vocal Christians can't seem to shut up about trying to "save" people or bring people into the flock. (male, 26–35, some college)

> People who are really religious or evangelical, I think—I tend to think—that they've never just actually stopped and thought. They're so busy proselytizing, they've never actually thought about what they're saying. (Riley)

> Those who are vocal Christians are proselytizers and already know beyond all doubt that theirs is the only right way. There is no rational discussion possible with these people because they feel that to entertain an opinion contrary to their rigid doctrinal ideology is nothing short of temptation by Satan himself, and is not to be given even the slightest entertainment by the mind for fear of losing one's soul. (male, 46–55, doctorate)

On the surface it is easy to see why atheists may find such efforts annoying. They have settled in their minds that religion is a farce and do not want to hear about such nonsense. But their irritation may go beyond what they consider rudeness. For some atheists, such interpersonal contact is an inappropriate way to change society. This is a realistic perception, given that atheists see efforts at emotional indoctrination as ways of keeping people from thinking rationally. Atheists are suspicious of proselytizing and instead support rational efforts to alter social structures since they contend that the former efforts are more reliant on emotional manipulation. One of our interview subjects indicated this reluctance to proselytize by stating, "I don't really evangelize atheism because it is simply a lack of religion. What I would say is all I really want people to do is continue their search for the actual truth and not allow people to spoon-feed it to them" (Elaine). Rather than turning to evangelism, this respondent hoped that individuals will rationally discover the truth. In this context, it becomes easier to understand why atheists have such a visceral reaction against proselytization, as those efforts can be seen as shortcutting the intellectual engagement that can lead to atheism. Some atheists even see such efforts as an example of unwarranted intrusion into the lives of others rather than as an effort to engage in discourse about spiritual reality.

> *Interviewer*: What do you mean by imposing—
> *Interviewee*: Proselytizing, trying to convert people into their way of thinking and saying your way of thinking, you're going to go to hell and all that kind of thing. (Teresa)

> I don't want anyone in my face with their proselytizing which they would be unable to stop. We would end up in a major argument. (female, 66–75, master's degree)

> Keep your religion to yourself. Proselytizing should be forbidden and punishable by imprisonment. Inmates should be exposed to large, daily doses of logic and reason so they can return to society as rational, thinking people. (male, 46–55, some college)

Atheism in the United States is a politicized movement. It is through these political efforts that atheists hope to make alterations to our society. Previous work has looked at how religious orientation leads to political activism.[7] The connection between religious beliefs and political attitudes is well established. Thus, it is not surprising that irreligious belief would also be connected to political attitudes. Beliefs about the supernatural speak to ideas about how we should organize our society. Since our sample only contains atheists, we are not in a position to make claims about whether atheists are more politicized than their religious out-groups. However, it does seem that atheism is at least as politicized as conservative religious faiths. Given the passion many of our respondents exhibited for their political causes, it is hard to envision how religious individuals could be more politicized than our atheist respondents. Ideally, future quantitative research will document the degree of political activism of atheists relative to those of more traditional religious preferences.

Chapter Six

Toward an Atheist Morality

It can be argued that the idea of morality has been co-opted by traditional religionists. The need for morality is one of the motivations some advocates of traditional religion use to justify religious support.[1] Under the rubric of traditional religion, morality is seen as the willingness to adhere to the commands of an overarching deity. If we define morality in this manner, then those not believing in a deity, much less those who are not willing to obey this deity, cannot be seen as moral individuals. However, such obedience is not the only way to construct morality. Since they cannot be conceived of as moral individuals in a traditional religious understanding of morality, atheists have an important social interest in constructing a different way for understanding morality. How they construct this different morality is the focus of this chapter.

WHAT IS MORALITY?

A very basic question is: What is morality? One of the *Webster New World Dictionary* definitions of morality is that it is the "rightness or wrongness of an action." The dictionary also states that morality is "being in accord with moral principles." These definitions are a good starting point to look more closely at how a concept of morality serves a culture and/or subculture. Morality provides a set of right actions and wrong actions. It justifies or opposes those actions by tying them to larger principles. In this way morality tells individuals in a society what they need to do to be considered a good person, and it also defines who is bad. The principles inform us as to why certain actions are good or bad. Thus, morality is important for providing a certain degree of social control. While individuals may be disturbed by the notion of society controlling them, few individuals really wish to live in a society of true anarchy. Such a society, where the most heinous of actions would be seen as no different from the most positive actions, would create a degree of chaos disrupting the social and legal stability most people desire.

For this reason, a sense of right and wrong (or morality, if one is more comfortable with that term) is a cultural universal. What is moral can vary greatly from society to society, as there is clear variation in the moral principles actions are based upon. But all societies and subcultures have a sense of what is right and what is wrong. In the past, justification for morality was rooted in the acceptance of otherworldly forces that provided a set of moral rules. As some societies have become more secular, deciding how to justify new modes of morality has become an enduring challenge. This challenge falls upon atheists in the United States.

One of the struggles of atheism has been to determine a source of morality without relying on the existence of a deity. This was a major topic of classical atheist philosophers.[2] Generally philosophers have argued that moral assertions have to be based on forces beyond the human to have sufficient legitimization. Fully struggling with this dilemma from a philosophical perspective is an enormous topic requiring more attention than we can give it and is beyond the scope of this work. Suffice it to say that one of the criticisms of atheism is that it naturally leads to anarchy since it becomes impossible to move beyond extreme moral relativism. Given this criticism, we are interested in how the average atheist in the United States constructs his or her notion of morality without a reliance on supernatural entities. That individual may not be acquainted with the larger philosophical arguments surrounding atheism and moral relativism, but he or she still must struggle with assertions of right and wrong without relying on a deity to provide direction. Our work in chapter 5 indicates an important way in which such individuals may justify their moral assertions. The application of progressive political ideals potentially provides atheists with a set of values and demands that allows them to construct rules of right and wrong that fit into their nonreligious worldview. It is important to listen to our respondents with an ear as to how they exhibit a new politically based morality comporting with their atheism.

THE POLITICAL MORALITY OF ATHEISM

We have seen evidence that atheists are heavily tied to progressive political ideology. To understand how atheists shape their moral underpinning, we have to consider the role played by their political orientation. Without a belief in the supernatural, atheists must look to moral forces in the material world to identify values and moral rules. People of supernatural faith can hope for a utopian world to come. Atheists have to hope for the creation of a utopia in the here and now. With such an expectation, atheists envision a better world for our future toward which we *must* progress. Creating this better world is the basis of atheist morality.

To understand what we need for this better world, atheists have to conceptualize what this world looks like. We have already established that atheists tend to see religion as foolishness. The type of social world atheists want us to head toward would naturally be one where the importance of religion is downplayed or even eliminated. This implies a secular society instead of one in which religion motivates individuals and/or social actions. Many of our respondents extolled the potential virtues of a secular society.

> So I would prefer to see a more secular society where we don't have the blurring of the lines between separation of church and state that we seem to have today in this country and many other countries. I would prefer to see government run in a completely secular fashion the way I think that the framers of our constitution designed it to be without the blurring of the lines that we see today. (Bill)

> I think the Christian Right threatens the United States' secular principles by trying, and sometimes succeeding, to incorporate Christian doctrine into our laws. They are a dangerous group that looks for moral guidance from primitive, ancient scripture rather than using rational, intellectual thought. (male, 26–35, master's degree)

> Separation of Church and State. Freedom FROM religion. I don't understand why our politicians re-interpret the constitution and get involved with religion anyway? No involvement whatsoever of the State and religion. Why do the two have to be connected? Why can't we have a strictly secular government? (male, 46–55, some graduate school)

Some of our respondents already see a movement toward a secular society and are quite pleased with that possibility. These respondents envision a progression in which the irrationality of religion fades further into the background and atheism, or at least secular philosophies, bring on a new era of enlightenment. Some look to Europe as a template for our future.

> I just hope that in the future that everybody's points of view will be respected rather than just a few people's points of view. I think we're moving in that direction. Certainly Europe has. We used to live in France. The Pope came over when we were there and just blasted the French. . . . French churches are certainly empty, except for funerals and weddings. (Nicole)

> Christian fundamentalism is losing ground in England, Europe, Australia, Canada, and South America as people become better educated. When Christianity finally disappears from North America in the next few decades, we can

get on with the business of living in a natural, rational world and watch the "supernatural world" disappear. (male, 66–75, bachelor's degree)

However, not all atheists are optimistic that this future will come. Many believe that whether we reach this new era of enlightenment is up for grabs. Therefore, it is important to them that proper efforts are made to ensure that we will one day be free from irrational religion. Religion must be combated and resisted. The manner in which these atheists seek to combat religion generally focuses on limiting the ability of religion to invade our government and to indoctrinate children through our educational system. In chapter 5 we observed how these were two institutions on which atheists focused much of their political energy. It is not surprising that atheists also embed certain moral values in having a "rational" governmental and educational system.

For atheists, the proper governmental system is free from religion. This leads them to transforming the term "separation of church and state" into a sacred concept. We have already noted that this term can have a variety of meanings for different individuals. But the value of church/state separation is held to be unassailable by many of our respondents.

I consider the Christian Right to be the primary threat to the continued existence of a secular United States. The United States is the most religiously diverse society in the world, primarily because the government has kept its hands off of religion and because religion has (barely) kept its hands off of government. (male, 66–75, some college)

Mostly because I don't want my government—it scares me that the government is so inundated with people who want to bless me and want God to bless me. I find that—that hurts my heart when I hear elected officials say, "God bless you." Please don't say that. That's so divisive. (Debra)

The value of church/state separation is that it can be used to limit, or outright deny, access of governmental power to religious individuals. Thus atheists talk in moral terms, in terms of right and wrong, as they discuss the excesses of religion in government.

I think our nation is in great danger as it is, but I think it's particularly dangerous to have people with deep religious convictions having power in our government. I think that's wrong, and I think it's absolutely not what the founding fathers and mothers had in mind. (Nicole)

I'm also very uncomfortable with a lot of the other ways that the religion has been seeping into the government lately . . . the way that religion affects our public schools . . . even though my daughter goes to a private school and I'm no longer a teacher, I am—I try to be active . . . I'll sign a petition, or send off a letter, or something like that. So, I'm concerned about it. (Judy)

The Christian Right is just plain wrong. They want to impose their misguided beliefs on everyone and will stop at nothing to change this country into a religious, dogma-driven theocracy that is intolerant of dissent. (male, 36–45, high school diploma)

Note how these respondents do not merely disagree with religious intrusion but also discuss it as a religious person might discuss the concept of sin. To such individuals, it is a poison that is wrong for society and must be combated with great moral fervor. Given the atheists' affinity for structuralism, preserving a secular government is seen as an important way to fix societal problems. A religious and irrational government is seen as having serious repercussions throughout society and must be resisted at all costs.

Education is another institution in which atheists have developed a moral interest. For atheists, education is the way to further promote science, and they tend to see education and science as one important dimension to be preserved from undue religious influence. It was common for our respondents to enumerate fears about this potential religious invasion of education and science.

I really think the anti-scientific perspectives that are involved really are hamstringing our development as a progressive, enlightened society. (Bruce)

My biggest issue is their interference in public education, especially their insistence that biblically-based creation stories be given equal time with the teaching of evolution. (female, 56–65, doctorate)

As long as religious beliefs are kept personal and are not forced into our government, I have no problem with people believing what they want. However, when that religious belief starts to intrude on my life, starts to hinder public education, or threatens to turn our country down the path to a theocracy, I have a huge problem. The Christian Right tends (lately) to want to do just that. Whether it's teaching ID/Creationism in public schools, denying climate change, being generally anti-science, opposing reproductive rights and healthcare, opposing stem-cell research, or just attempting to force Christianity on everyone else, the Christian Right is holding this country back or, in some ways, dragging this country down. (male, 36–45, bachelor's degree)

However, the interest of atheists was not merely in protecting these institutions but also in what these institutions could produce if run in a proper manner. For them, education and science are keys to eventually creating a secular, progressive world resembling their ideal society.

We need more money spent on secular education, so less people become religious bigots. (male, 46–55, master's degree)

I mean, we're getting into a stage where people are going to need to know more and more about science and technology, and the way the universe actually is. . . . I mean, if the electorate can't make informed decisions about science policy and education then I think we're setting ourselves up for a fall. (Albert)

I see them as anti-science, anti-progress and against ideas and values that would push the country forward. Their stand on gay rights and evolution are two perfect examples of this. (male, 46–55, bachelor's degree)

For the atheist, science and education will save us. These institutions are seen as capable of bringing in a new time of enlightenment if we can just prevent them from being corrupted by religion. Once again atheist morality is tied to making certain a given social structure—education—is organized in such a way to produce the desired secular society.

Atheists feel free to see themselves as moral in that they seek societal good through alteration of social structures rather than obedience to outdated moral standards. The alterations of social structures fit with their ideals of structuralism. The right social structures make for a better society, and therefore it is moral to fight for those social structures. Immorality is seen in attempting to maintain traditional and what are considered irrational structures. Atheists did not have any problems pointing out such acts of immorality as they saw them.

You know you go back, almost any of those early civilizations had a very strong religious base that was a part of the control structure to keep people either in poverty or keep people under the power of the rulers. (Dan)

They are hypocrites. They think they have the moral high ground and are superior to me, yet they turn a blind eye to deaths attributed to a lack of health care and to immoral, unnecessary wars. (female, 56–65, master's degree)

And Hispanic countries—Colombia and Latin America—third world countries are very, very susceptible to be influenced by, by evangelists and religious people because of all of what is going in our countries like poverty and injustice and all this stuff. So people are very, very vulnerable, and they tend to believe lies in order to get some kind of imaginary comfort. (Leroy)

It is unfortunate that so many people are unable to take charge of their own lives and feel the need to live under authoritarian social structures. The worst part is that it is at the more extreme edges of these social structures that extremists are created, of course not just in Christendom, but in many religions, and these extremists are willing to murder and die in pursuit of false gods and false afterlives. (male, 46–55, master's degree)

Much of traditional morality is focused on the actions of individuals. For atheists, altering social structures takes precedence over individual actions.

However, it would be misleading to state that individual actions are completely unimportant to atheists. Many of them condemn certain actions of religious individuals. Understanding the individual actions atheists condemn helps us to further comprehend atheist morality.

BAD ACTS ACCORDING TO ATHEISTS

It is tempting to limit the notion of morality of atheists to efforts at changing social structures. While clearly the political focus of atheists leads to an emphasis on correcting social structures, it would be a mistake to not also consider those actions of religious individuals that atheists consider immoral. These perceptions are built on the images of religious individuals that atheists have developed and are part of their larger critique of people with faith. Religion's irrationality is seen as compelling individuals toward actions that disrupt efforts to create positive social structures and promote social progress.

Atheists perceive the development of their unbelief as the result of their rational assessment. We illustrated the existence of particularism within many atheists. They simply do not understand how individuals have come to conclusions about the presence of a supernatural being that differ from the atheists' own conclusions. Several of our respondents were highly critical of religious individuals for their inability to logically think about their own religious ideas.

> Their ideals are based on a book that was created by man, not God, therefore what they are fighting for is man-made, not God ordained. Their inability to find answers to the questions that surround the glaring contradictions in the bible, and not just take their religious leaders' "word" for it. They don't think on their own. They listen. They regurgitate. (male, 26–35, some college)

> It doesn't take me very long in those rare conversations I might have with a believer that wants to go into it, it doesn't take me very long to where the believer says, "Well, it's just about faith." I give—the very best believer I give three or four minutes with me before they have to go to faith. Religion just doesn't stand up to typical, rational, reasonable arguments. (Bernard)

> By their irrationality shall ye know them . . . they sometimes lock themselves in their prayer towers and say that if people don't send 8 million, god is calling them home I fear irrational people they are not logical and they are very frustrating and a waste of time while they are brain washed like that. (male, 56–65, bachelor's degree)

It was common for our respondents to consider themselves courageous thinkers, whereas religious individuals were those afraid to fully consider the implications of their beliefs. It was common for atheists to envision religious individuals as fearful of testing their faith with logic and being unable to truly understand that there is no evidence for their religious beliefs. A typical comment comes from Ramon, who stated, "They're [religious individuals] afraid, they have their identity and don't want it shaken up." Thus, for many respondents, there was an immorality in the limited ways that religious individuals were willing to engage in critical thinking.

Some respondents argued that this inability developed due to how religious individuals were socialized. Many atheists believe that seemingly rational individuals coming to seemingly illogical conclusions is explained by the notion that there had to be a brainwashing that brought them to this position. The idea of brainwashing was fairly common among the respondents.

> I oppose religion as described because it is the brainwashing of the masses that leads to science, reason and logic being left behind. Nothing is right because it is written in a book, it must be proven by evidence and logic. (male, 66–75, doctorate)

> Because the brainwash is so strong that even women don't even ask that. They don't ask themselves like, hey, what about if God is a woman? (Leroy)

> They are the product of long established brainwashing from infancy—and they are too lazy to do the research and independent thought to find out for themselves the fiction of their "beliefs." (male, 66–75, some graduate school)

As such, atheists could relieve some religious individuals of responsibility for their erroneous thinking since it was embedded in them before they knew better. This allowed atheists to feel good about themselves, since those who grew up in religious homes conceptualized themselves as having been strong enough to overcome this brainwashing. This can be seen in the life of Rick. Rick was one of our younger interviewees (a graduate student in his mid-twenties). He grew up in a Christian family and stated that he did not have any doubts about his Christian faith as he grew up. In fact, when he went to college he planned to criticize the arguments of nonbelievers. He determined that "by the time we got through with college, we would understand what the flaws were and the scientific reasoning, and we'd construct the killer argument to defend our beliefs, and we would write a book about it or something when we got out."

However, once he arrived at college he found that he was not very successful in defending his faith. In fact, he began to develop doubts, as it seemed to him that a world without God or gods made more sense to him than his previous beliefs. He decided to think about what the world would look like without a deity and compare it to our actual world.

> And so this went on for a couple of weeks of pretty solid thinking, and I came to the conclusion that it was surprisingly sensical [*sic*] to view the world in that way and I didn't see any problems with it. And I decided that in fact, it took a bigger leap to see things the way I used to see things.

Over the course of six or seven months, Rick went from someone who was strongly religious to a confirmed atheist. As he sees it, he was able to learn to see the world as it really was.

But what about those who do not come to the same conclusion as Rick? We asked him why belief in the supernatural continues in our world. He started his explanation with themes of socialization: "As a young child, you have an authority figure that you look up to, and you trust in to make sure that things turn out all right for you. And when you're on your own, later on in life, it's tempting to reinvent that figure and just make it bigger." Rick went on to discuss the way traditions developed to reinforce religions came from a desire for a larger and in-control authority figure. For Rick, religion becomes a powerful force into which children are "indoctrinated." To overcome this indoctrination, one has to "get into certain circumstances" or be "innately open-minded enough to try to consider other things." With this statement Rick positions himself among those who believe themselves open-minded enough to see the folly of religion and appreciate objective reality. He develops positive sentiment about his atheism, as it is a means by which he is able to overcome the social forces pushing people into religion. For Rick, religion is an institution brainwashing individuals into irrational beliefs. Atheists view morality as individuals being strong enough to overthrow this brainwashing so as to see a reality they perceive to be objective.

However, the idea of brainwashing also leads to another personal moral issue for atheists. Even if some atheists had sympathy for those brainwashed, they had no sympathy for those who did the brainwashing. We noted in an earlier book that some cultural progressives perceived the leaders, rather than the followers, of conservative religious political movements as the villains.[3] Some of the atheists shared that sentiment. But beyond seeing political leaders as part of a societal problem, some atheists were also concerned with how children were being raised in their families of origin. How religion is brought into a child's life is a point of contention for some atheists.

> There should also be a law against brainwashing children. And laws that give a child the right to a sound education that teaches the wealth of knowledge we now have at our disposal, not just desirable bits and pieces. (male, 36–45, bachelor's degree)

> I think that there should be more books out there. I can't get enough. I think there should be books for children. The religious indoctrinate the kids as early as possible. (Lenny)

> They should be required to teach evolution to their children. Their children
> should be required to take sex education courses. (male, 66–75, doctorate)

The fear of children being indoctrinated into religion fits with the atheistic notion that religion is irrational and will disappear if people are given a fair chance to rationally think about it. This was one of the few areas where atheists had what could be considered an intrusive attitude toward people of faith. While not all atheists felt this way, some did exhibit regret that religious individuals were allowed to socialize (or, in their eyes, indoctrinate) their children into religion and questioned whether such individuals should be allowed to continue to do so. While generally atheists emphasized that people should be basically free to believe as they want and conduct their family life as they wish, this was one area where atheists talked about intrusion. This exception indicates the strength of the concerns atheists have about religious training.[4] Atheists exhibit a powerful sense of immorality as it concerns influencing one's child to accept a religious faith since it helps perpetuate the religious ideology that they see as making our society worse.

Even though atheists look with disdain on these individual actions, they have not completely neglected their propensity for structuralism. If we look toward what atheists consider to be personal "sins," they pertain to the inability of individuals to participate in the changes that society needs or to blockage of the changes atheists desire. Atheists conceptualize individuals who do not come to the same conclusions about religion that they have as not having thought deeply enough about such issues and as not being fully developed in their thinking patterns. Such individuals may be thought of as being "backward" and may inhibit movement toward a progressive, secular society. Likewise, atheists fear that the way children are socialized will help perpetuate religion by creating future cohorts of spiritual followers. The "sin" of indoctrinating one's children into religion exacerbates the problems created by religion since it means that secularists will have to deal with religious believers for the foreseeable future. Atheists hope to see the day when religion becomes irrelevant, and they see whatever postpones us from experiencing that day as wrong and immoral.

The morality of atheists is fairly silent concerning how people live their own lives. We have noted the one exception to this trend in the resentment that some atheists harbor toward those who socialize their children in religious faith. Furthermore, a few atheists believe that traditional morality may not be a healthy lifestyle since it leads to sexual repression. However, atheists in general were very tolerant of the life choices individuals make and simply asked that they be left alone to make their own life choices. In this sense there was not a powerful component of atheist morality regarding how individuals conducted their own lives. Only if those individuals' actions threatened the emergence of a new secular society were they condemned by most atheists.

TOWARD A MORALITY WITHOUT GOD

The argument that atheists are not moral individuals is not supported by our respondents' comments. Contrary to what some religious individuals believe, atheism is not generally used to excuse individuals from having the responsibility for determining right and wrong. Most respondents clearly spoke about the concept of good and evil as they saw it in our society. However, the rules of morality in an atheist system do vary from the rules of morality in a traditionally religious system. They are based on the presupposition of the dysfunction of religion and the assertion that rationality, rather than religion, should be the organizing principle of society. This leads to an overarching moral principle of political progressiveness and to attempts to create rational social structures. In spite of the philosophical argument that moral assertions not based on a system external to humans cannot be defended, atheists conceive of a moral system that ties much of that morality to their political, rather than theological, concerns.

Atheist morality is a system focused on creating a better society by altering the social structures that hold society back and keep society in a primitive culture. Their de-emphasis of personal actions speaks to an attitude less likely to be judgmental of individual behavior. For this reason, it is easy to see the morality of atheism as one of tolerance and not a proclamation of right and wrong. This would be a mistake. Many of our respondents clearly had powerful ideas about what they saw as right and wrong in society. Individuals who were seen as getting in the way of achieving the desired secular culture were often belittled and stigmatized by our respondents from the online survey.[5]

> They are mental retards. They are against abortion, science and reason. They want to use their advantages to dictate the political agenda in America. (male, over 75, doctorate)

> Can we put them in the same building with all the fundamentalist Muslims and fundamentalist Jews, and close the doors and let them all fight it out amongst themselves? I wish they would go away. They are misguided and stand in the way of environmental, social, and political progress. They are anti-intellectual and often an embarrassment to the United States. (female, 36–45, some graduate school)

> Fear-mongering persons who refuse to live in reality, and who bow and scrape to an invisible, make-believe man in the sky, in hopes that he will keep them from having to face the inevitability of death. Frankly it is a childish, ugly,

short-sighted outlook and worldview, and one that generally appears to attempt to hold back human progress and oppress women, gays and other minorities. (male, 26–35, doctorate)

There is a definite demonizing by atheists of those seen as barriers to
progress. Atheists may not be highly judgmental concerning personal actions, but they are judgmental when it comes to dealing with religious, conservative attitudes.

The hostility atheists have toward out-group members indicates that even
morality systems based on notions of tolerance draw boundaries that must be
defended. The best way to defend those boundaries is often to decide who is
not part of the in-group and to stigmatize those individuals. Atheists face
more stigma than people with religious beliefs,[6] and yet they do not show
hesitation at demonizing those who do not agree with them. Out-group rejection may be a cultural universal since it is in this rejection that groups are
able to define themselves and establish what they want. Atheists want a
secular society, and since some religious and conservative individuals stand
in the way of that society, it is natural for atheists to reject them.

The eagerness of atheists to create a secular society can be seen in some
of the public actions of atheist organizations. For example, these groups
often launch court cases concerning public religious displays that may seem
rather innocuous. Most people do not envision a roadside cross or a display
of the Ten Commandments as attempts to indoctrinate individuals into religion. But their presence is a reminder of the religious values many people
attribute to our society. In this way such icons are symbolic reminders to
atheists of an unwanted religious presence. Another unwanted religious presence is the words "In God We Trust" written on our money. Many of our
respondents commented on the undesirability of such symbols, and we
should not be surprised by the numerous lawsuits that outright atheist (e.g.,
the Freedom from Religion Foundation) and sympathetic (e.g., Americans
United for the Separation of Church and State) organizations launch to re-
move such symbols. Furthermore, some atheist organizations put up billboards aimed at convincing more individuals of the foolishness of religion.
Whether these billboards have an effect is beyond the scope of this current
study. But they do represent the desire of atheists to increase unbelief and
hasten the development of a secular society. While many atheists tend to
reject personal evangelizing for atheism, they still do not mind the public
presence of such billboards that they obviously hope will bring more atheists
into their social movement.

In the morality of atheists we begin to see the future they envision. Atheists are not of one mind regarding the place of religion in society. Some want
it removed completely, while others are willing to tolerate it as long as
religion does not interfere with their lives and their government. However,

just about all of them want it to have less influence as they conceptualize a society in which secular rationality is the basis for decision-making in the public sector. If religion is allowed, it will only be in the private domain of individual homes and religious buildings. Proselytizing will be highly discouraged and stigmatized. A progressive government that counters many of the shortcomings of capitalism is seen as a rational part of this society, along with the freedom to construct one's family and sexual expectations as one sees fit. In an atheist's morality, anything seen as interfering with the development of such a society is immoral while whatever speeds up the development of this society is moral. Religion has been conceptualized as a barrier to this desired societal destination and generally deemed immoral. In reality, atheists are just as moral as people of faith but they see themselves as having a different, and more advanced, idea of morality than their religious peers.

The moral ideals of atheists do not operate in isolation from other important social forces. After all, atheists are a subset of a larger group of cultural progressives who espouse many of the same concerns enunciated by our respondents. Other cultural progressives may not be as certain regarding the nonexistence of deities as our respondents are, but their vision of an ideal society is not highly different from that of our respondents. This similarity of goals and visions is important since atheists are still a distinct numerical minority in the United States and are likely to remain relatively low in numbers for the foreseeable future. Thus atheists operate within a movement of other cultural progressive activists in an effort to achieve common goals. Atheists may serve an important purpose in supplying an argument against the theological implications of their political foes, as the contention of atheists of the nonexistence of the deity makes it more difficult to conceptualize a society where rules and mores can be based on notions of a deity. So while they are merely a part of a larger movement of cultural progressive activists, atheists clearly are important to that movement.

Chapter Seven

Atheism in the United States

The religious landscape in contemporary America is very, very complex, and finding atheists, who make up a very small percentage of the population, is difficult at best, as are efforts to generalize findings of a single study to all atheists. We understand our limitations and so will be modest in our efforts to make sense of atheism's place in and effects on the larger religious/nonreligious profile of the United States. What we have done is this: Find people who self-identify as atheists in different regions of the United States and who, in their own words, can give us some insight into their minds and motivations, especially regarding what characteristics of contemporary religion in the United States they find threatening and in need of negation. Comparing responses of atheists in strategically different regions of the United States may give us a chance to test contact theory and explore the nature of the dialectic between religion and atheism and the paths that lead atheists to their beliefs.

Viewing atheism as an attempt to negate the effects of religion, we believe a good place to start is with a profile of religion in the United States.[1] With that established, perhaps we can see approximately what it is that modern atheism is attempting to negate. What groups, messages, and movements threaten the worldviews and ideologies of atheists? Central to this exploration will be the assumption that control and conflict are central to the dialectic between atheism and religion. If so, we should expect that struggles ultimately will be over scarce resources that both sides desire, and threats to the acquisition of those resources that pose a major problem and identify potential enemies.

According to Gallup polls,[2] in 2011 approximately 92 percent of Americans professed a belief in God. That compares to 96 percent, according to polls conducted in 1944,[3] so the overwhelming majority of Americans do believe in God, however envisioned. In the strict sense of the term, Americans have been, and continue to be, a religious people. However, as we look more closely at the nature of their beliefs and affiliations, we find some things of interest that may help us explain the apparent recent growth in atheism and the increase in those who may be religious but have no religious affiliation—the nones. With belief in God almost constant over the last sixty-plus years, that number alone does not help us understand the reason for recent increases in the number of atheists or the number of nones.

Earlier we stated that conservative Christianity in the United States has been growing as more progressive, mainstream denominations have been in decline. While both of these statements are true, it is also true that the number of Americans who call themselves fundamentalists declined from a high of 36 percent in 1987 to 30 percent in 2004,[4] and the number of Americans who self-identify as atheists increased.[5] Bruce Hunsberger and Bob Altemeyer concluded that extreme messages about religion, irreligion, and substantive issues like homosexuality have driven many from the ranks of the religious to the category of individuals known as the nones. If so, then it may have been the movement toward conservatism that made critical thinkers eventually depart from fundamentalist positions to relativism and then perhaps from apostasy to atheism altogether.

While we do not know exactly if or how this is related to a parallel growth in atheists, or at least those who are willing to self-identify as atheists, it may be that there is a whole continuum of people who are moving from conservative religion to nominal religion, to no religion, and then possibly on to nonbelief. Certainly we heard from atheists in this study who grew up in families that were nominally religious and who had epiphanies later on that convinced them of atheism's validity. However, without more objective data, this is only speculation. Another possibility is that there has always been a substantial number of Americans who are technically atheists, and the contemporary climate of inclusion and emphasis on individual rights has emboldened more to own that identity publicly.

One influential study identified two general factors that led to apostasy, or at least the apostasy-to-none status: (1) strong religious training producing people who highly value truth and integrity, and (2) highly intelligent children being freer and more able to critically analyze religious beliefs, making them confident in their judgment of religion.[6] In that study, most of the subjects were nones, not atheists. In fact, another study concluded that there are actually very few apostates from religion to atheism among the nones.[7] Atheists, they argued, are a rare breed and very difficult to find. For this reason, we believe, it is important to get not just quantifiable data but also stories and meanings, and so we took up this effort to allow atheists to speak for themselves.

Regardless of labels and types, it is fairly clear that modern society is more pluralistic than ever, that one of the fastest growing groups in terms of religion is the nones, and that atheists in the United States are living in a society more open to their inclusion than ever before. True, they still are not well trusted, but they exist in a social system that supports inclusion and is used to marginalized groups claiming their public voices.[8] Leaders have emerged, behind whom atheists have gathered, confident that others have articulated what they would if they could.

THE RELIGION THAT CONTEMPORARY AMERICAN ATHEISTS ARE ATTEMPTING TO NEGATE

In our chapter 2 review of relevant events in the history of atheism we stopped just short of what we take up in this chapter: a review of the status of religion in contemporary American society and a discussion of its character- istics that atheists might feel need to be countered and negated. Exactly what is it that feels most threatening to atheists about the beliefs and actions of America's religious communities? First, let's review some historical high- lights that put today's conflict into perspective.

The debate between religion and atheism has deep historical roots. In its earliest form atheism was simply an accusatory moniker that individuals leveled at others who did not believe in or respect *their* God or gods, who accompanied them in battle and abstractly represented the group.[9] It appar- ently was the case in most premodern societies that everyone believed in something other, something holy, something sacred. Political, social, and economic wars were fought between groups with different forms of religion, and deities were used to justify war and celebrate victory. It was not the people who were victorious; instead, the God or gods who were with them were credited with the victory, and derision of the gods of the losers was common.

Not until the eighteenth century was the term "atheist" owned by free thinkers and those who publicly objected to the rules and abuses of religion, especially those of Roman Catholicism in Western Europe. French social philosophers such as Diderot claimed the title of atheist for themselves as they appealed to reason and denounced religion as chimera or superstition. In intellectual circles this emphasis on rationality and, eventually, science began to displace religious explanations of the cosmos and particularly of human societies.[10] Because Roman Catholicism was enmeshed with political author- ity, many of these atheistic social philosophers were opposed by political leaders and, at times, imprisoned. But the masses of nonintellectuals appar- ently continued to accept religious explanations of the natural world. This was particularly true in the emerging United States.

Through the nineteenth and early twentieth centuries the debate grew more heated, especially as science began to have more and more social and economic payoffs. Even the religious, however, tended to accept intellectuals and scientists who were believed to make valuable contributions to society or provide help in war, such as the nuclear physicists who built the first atomic bomb that contributed to the close of World War II in the Pacific theater.[11] For a short period of time intellectuals were our heroes, although soon the association of the term "atheist" with the pejorative labels "communist," "intellectual," and "anti-American" once again caused Americans to distrust anyone who was suspected of being an atheist, which apparently is still true to some extent to this day.[12]

Overall, religion maintained its grip on the American population, with belief in God or a supreme being consistently found to be the norm among Americans as we headed into the second half of the twentieth century.[13] The first noticeable change occurred, not surprisingly, when many other parts of American society began to change in the 1960s. While the percentage of those who reported a belief in God remained high and fairly consistent for most of the second half of the twentieth century and into the beginning of the twenty-first, those who opted for alternatives to the existing traditions in the definition of God and the formal organizations of religion began to increase. As mentioned earlier, this was a time when we experienced growth among religious switchers, among the nones, and (most recently) among atheists.[14]

At the same time other social changes were taking place, such as the emancipation of women and their entry into the labor force, the sexual revolution, the civil rights movement, acceptance of those with alternative ideas about the practice of religion, and eventually the rise of those with nontraditional sexual orientations (the lesbian, gay, bisexual, and transgender [LGBT] community). Previously marginalized groups and individuals began to stand up and claim their identities and their right to be fully acknowledged and integrated parts of American society. Religious pluralism paralleled the rise in social and moral pluralism. In contemporary America, individuals are faced with more than what Peter Berger once labeled the heretical imperative in which each person *must* choose, not just *may* choose, their own belief system and religion to follow. Each must also choose among competing views on the many social issues of the day.[15] This may be one of the things that explains why so many researchers have observed that "denomination" is less and less useful in defining the belief systems of a group of people. There is so much heresy (choosing to believe in ways that differ from the formally accepted teachings of one's denomination) within most denominations that the term has become almost meaningless.[16]

Concurrent with these developments was the flourishing of Christian fundamentalism, which aggressively opposed progressive ideas such as the theory of evolution and interpretation of the Bible as allegory and myth.[17] In mainstream Protestant Christianity, however, there was turmoil about whether and how to incorporate what appeared to be scientific fact with biblical tradition. Many denominations experienced splits, with progressives moving to the figurative left, incorporating less literal interpretations of scripture and more this-worldly theologies that emphasized human service and the expression of religiosity in the form of doing good in the world.

In most of these groups, however, were those who moved even further to the right, who clung even more tightly to a traditional, literal reading of scriptures and to practices more closely aligned with Christian fundamentalism. Those who moved to the left posed few problems to atheists because in many ways they shared some of the same ideas about social progress and the nature of a perfect society. Even if they disagreed on the supernatural world, in matters that had to do with the role of politics or the capacity of government to limit or restrict behavior, they had little conflict. Progressives, whether atheist or theist, share a morality and social agenda and become allies in the political arena. As stated earlier, the real source of religious conflict, or the conflict between theism and atheism, rarely has to do with belief systems themselves. Rather, the conflict usually has to do with power and control over rights and privileges, and it ultimately is played out in politics.

From this brief discussion we see how Christianity changed throughout the nineteenth and twentieth centuries, with science and rationality fragmenting even further an already denominationally divided society. In their response to evolutionary theory and threats to the literal truth of the Bible, many Christians became open to, and almost willing to accept, the preeminence of science as the arbiter of truth and therefore were vulnerable to the attacks of atheism. Broad progressive influences on American society soon began to affect religious institutions, with some individuals and groups embracing those influences while others were driven even more deeply into conservatism. The former eventually became political allies of atheists, while the latter became identified as an enemy.

THE CASE OF ANGLICANISM

One contemporary case study may bring these speculative arguments down to earth. The Anglican Communion is a worldwide network of churches that share similar traditions and liturgies based on those proclaimed and practiced by the Church of England since the sixteenth century. The real authority of the church is held by its bishops, the regional overseers (*episcopas*) who direct local priests and parishes. When they convene as colleges of bishops they have great authority to define the mission and official policies and theologies of Anglicanism, such as the ordination of women or the inclusion of homosexuals. The worldwide coordination and unity of Anglicanism is one of the principal jobs of the Archbishop of Canterbury, who is, among other things, "first among equals." He has never been given the equivalent of papal authority, and in many ways is just a bishop among bishops. He does, however, have perceived authority and the ability to convene all Anglican/Episcopalian bishops for the purpose of working through differences and establishing positions on social policy and ecclesiastical practices.

In the United States, Anglicanism took the name "Episcopal," acknowledging its basic structure of authority centered on the *episcopas*. In alternative names and forms Anglicanism spread, as did the British Empire, so that, ultimately, there was a time when the sun literally never set on the Anglican Communion. As communal as this sounds, keep in mind that the British Empire was, geographically, overrepresented by less developed countries in which science and Western forms of rationality had not yet taken hold. The eventual conflict is easy to see in hindsight.

Over the course of time, the Episcopal Church in the United States of America (ECUSA, also known as the Episcopal Church or TEC) came to be identified as the church of choice among elites. More presidents have been Episcopalians than have come from any other Christian denomination, and the first seven were from the state of Virginia, which had very close ties between religion (Anglicanism) and government. For a democratic society in which the separation of church and state has been idealized, this seems odd, especially today when less than 2 percent of Americans are Episcopalians. [18]

As a church of the elites, they also have been the religious choice of many intellectuals, opening themselves to a progressive ideology that has now explicitly stated its support for the inclusion of women and gays in the clergy as well as same-sex marriage. Among their clergy and most of their adherents, atheists find few enemies and, in many ways, close allies in their fight for the separation of church and state, more liberal and inclusive social policies, and the pursuit of economic and social justice for marginalized populations. And as with atheists, these progressive theists are now often associated with the political left.

ECUSA comfort with progressive ideals may best be seen in their election of the current presiding bishop, the Most Reverend Katharine Jefferts Schiori, who was invested as presiding bishop in 2006. Simply ordaining a woman to the priesthood was controversial, but investing a woman as first among equals in the entire ECUSA was an outrage for traditionalists. The progressive influence of a majority of American bishops indicated that the tide had turned and the majority of Episcopalians could now be considered progressives. What is equally indicative of this progressive, and therefore scientific, orientation is the fact that the Most Reverend Katharine Jefferts Schiori was not originally trained for the priesthood, but rather had a career as an oceanographer—a scientist—before her seminary training. The official website of the Episcopal Church[19] confirmed this reliance on science by having front and center on its home page in the summer of 2012 not quotes from scripture, but ones attributed to Nicolaus Copernicus and Johannes Kepler.

But in the global south, there were other things at work. Adherents to the Anglican tradition in the less developed world brought their traditionalism to their practice of religion and were joined by Anglicans and Episcopalians in the developed world who were traditionalists and sympathetic with their views. Much less affected by the progressive influences of Western civilization and much more entrenched in traditional views on matters such as human sexuality, they tended to be more closely aligned ideologically and theologically with those whom we might call fundamentalists.

To make things even more interesting, today a majority of worldwide Anglicans live in the developing world. More than thirty-eight million of the eighty million Anglicans in the world today live in Africa.[20] In the United States there are approximately two million and in Great Britain there are just over thirteen million.[21] However, their societies are impoverished and they are dependent on the charity of those with money. In this case, this happens to be those of the perceived apostasy of Communion members in more developed societies. So who has power, the dominant and wealthy (and largely heretical in the eyes of conservatives) minority or the conservative majority? Stay tuned for an answer to that question because we don't yet know.

These types of fights generally lead to a need to engage in fearmongering on both sides. Thus, the fears of both conservatives and progressives, or at least religious conservatives and atheists, are imaginary or at best inflated. The idea that religious conservatives could ever turn the United States into a theocracy is absurd, and the notion that progressives are un-American and immoral is without foundation.

What this discussion does emphasize, however, is that the public debate between atheists and theists is primarily between atheists and conservative or fundamentalist theists. With more progressive theists it seems there is little friction. Why? Because they share the same relationship to power and moral standards. Certainly they disagree as to the existence of a supreme being and possibly the spiritual nature of the cosmos. But they seem content to agree to disagree. Real conflict, public and heated conflict, is sparked when moral and political turf is at stake. The conservative end of the Anglican/Episcopalian spectrum is at odds with the goals and purposes of atheists, but the progressive end seems relatively content to let them be.

ATHEISM, CONTEMPORARY AMERICAN THEISMS, AND THEIR FORMS OF DEBATE

The current religious makeup of American society does not paint a picture of a monolithic enemy of atheism. It shows America to be a denominational society in which the term "Christian" is so broadly used that it is hardly useful in this analysis. It is largely a society of primarily Christian pluralism with extreme theological and social differences even within the same denomination. Regardless, America is still overwhelmingly religious.

In 2008, 76 percent of Americans self-identified as Christian, and 34 percent self-identified as born-again or evangelical. A total of 70 percent believed in a personal God,[22] and 12 percent were deists who believed in a God, just not one who was personal or who intervened in human history.[23] Mainline, progressive denominations were in decline, and conservative ones, especially nondenominational churches, were growing—in many cases rapidly. We should keep in mind that these statistics are broad, descriptive strokes, and unless we are careful we may wrongly assume that there is homogeneity within denominational groups. A case in point is the usefulness of the denominational label "Episcopalian." Under that rubric are fundamentalists and charismatics, Anglo-Catholics, evangelicals, and social and religious progressives.

It may be because of the inconsistency in progressivism and conservatism within Christian denominations and because the average members of these groups do not have a public voice or a platform from which to speak that selected individuals who do have such platforms in terms of television, radio, and the Internet seem to have disproportionately loud and influential voices. Many of the prominent politically conservative religious voices may also be interpreted as representative of Christianity. To the extent that atheists interpret these voices as representative of all Christians, their focus may be on the entirety of the Christian religion as they formulate ideas and strategies to negate its influence.

The Anglican example is at least one type of religious reality that atheism faces in the United States today. Religious progressives hardly show up on their radars, but conservatives and traditionalists are in their crosshairs and represent the religion that contemporary atheism attempts to negate. They are not in competition with progressives even if they are religious. As most of our respondents stated (especially those in the face-to-face interviews), if people want to believe what atheists see as the illogical and imaginary, it is their right to do so. But if people who are religious attempt to define society's boundaries and establish or reinforce moral boundaries on religious grounds, and especially if they attempt to do so through political influence, they become the enemy. We would argue that power and control are the central issues, and that the valuable and scarce resources fought over are the moral boundaries and constraints that are legislated by Congress and other political bodies.

Technically, we would argue, religion is not typically seen by atheists as an enemy; at its very best it is seen as merely a waste of time and a drag on social progress. As a public radio figure recently quoted a famous American technology mogul as saying, Sunday mornings are a huge waste of time when people could be productive, working toward innovation and creation rather than worshipping an imaginary creator. The individuals whose messages contemporary atheism *is* attempting to negate are Christian fundamentalists and traditionalists who are evangelizing, proselytizing, judging, and, of utmost importance, attempting to influence social policy and law.

One of the most interesting dimensions of this war between contemporary atheism and theism is the extent to which, as we just mentioned, it is played out via the media, and the extent to which these communities find encouragement, information, and identity through virtual communities online and via publications and the media. For example, remember the dramatic growth over the last few decades in organizations such as the Freedom from Religion Foundation discussed briefly in chapter 2. Their period of growth may be explained as a surge in the number of Americans who decided that they are atheists. It also may be true, however—and we suspect this to be the case— that their strong Web-based presence combined with the new culture of "coming out" have together created a new virtual community. It may not be an increase in the numbers of atheists at all. It may be a surge in the number of atheists who are willing to come out and find reassurance and other valuable social resources through virtual communities.

REGIONAL BATTLES OF ATHEISM AND RELIGION: THE BIBLE BELT VERSUS THE MIDWEST

Just as there are many forms of religion and almost countless versions of Christianity in the United States, so there are many regions and localities that have unique characteristics. We're all used to pundits and commentators referring to blue states and red states at election time. Those labels make sense, as historic patterns of voting confirm. Again, history has something to contribute to this phenomenon.

It is widely acknowledged that the South tends to be conservative and Republican. It also is widely acknowledged that other areas, such as the Northeast, are typically progressive and Democratic. Why is the South conservative? Ronald Johnstone argues that those who settled America's West and South tended to be people who were less educated and more likely to be members of fundamentalist denominations, predominantly Methodists and Baptists.[24] They were not among the privileged of the Northeast who had little reason to uproot their families for a better future and whose status quo was just fine, thank you very much. Those who were marginalized dreamed of a better place where they could own their land and move up the social and economic ladder. They were the ones who uprooted and sought something better. They were the ones who settled the South and whose influence is still felt. And they were disproportionately traditionalists and conservatives.

The fundamentalists and conservatives who built the South found a literal interpretation of the Bible a convenient source of rationalization for economic practices including slavery. The Bible never overtly outlaws slavery; it never identifies it as an economic arrangement that is forbidden to God's followers, even in the New Testament. It simply describes how slaves should be treated and proscribes abuse and mistreatment. This interpretation with its associated economic motivation is part of what split the Methodist Church around the time of the Civil War and is the reason why to this day there is a denomination known as the Southern Methodists as well as a Southern Methodist University. The lesson to be learned is that religion, like all social institutions, cannot be understood as something unto itself. It is woven into a social fabric, and every social institution—including the economy, family, and education—is part and parcel of the same social fabric. Each affects the others. So a regional comparison is called for in order to test these ideas as well as the proposal that social contact may also affect religious attitudes.

Does regional variation in religious conservatism affect the attitudes and opinions of atheists regarding their own beliefs, religion in general, and evangelicals and fundamentalists in particular? Are atheists in very conservative areas such as the Bible Belt less likely to "come out," or are they more aggressive because their religious environment is perceived to be more hostile? In one study little difference was found between San Francisco atheists and those from Alabama in terms of dogmatism and zeal, although there was a significant difference in their preference for public schools to teach their beliefs.[25] Atheists in Alabama outnumbered San Francisco atheists almost three-to-one in the desire for their beliefs to be taught in public schools. The study provided little elaboration, but it could be that the Alabama atheists' attitudes reflected a greater felt need to counter the influences of Christian teachings in local public schools.

To attempt to answer these questions we selected one group from an area that is known to be progressive and the other from a Bible Belt area. We acknowledge that this presents problems for the generalization of our findings to the total American population, but at least we do have variations across at least two different regions of the country, so we have been able to test our contact hypothesis. However, our approach was unique in that it focused on open-ended questions and face-to-face interviews. Using this method allowed atheists to tell us their stories and elaborate on their impressions, meanings, and motives. It also allowed us to get more history as to how each respondent developed the atheistic views he or she had at the time of the interview or survey.

Our findings show some clear differences between Midwestern atheists and those from the Bible Belt. The latter are more likely to have previously been religious, to have grown up in a religious home, to have had religious friends while growing up, and to have become atheists at a younger age. They also were more likely to have grown up in low-income homes and to have experienced conflict in those homes.

Atheists from the Bible Belt were less likely to complain about religion and less likely to fear theocracy or an aggressive dominance by those who were religious, although they were concerned with the intolerance of religious individuals and what they saw as their tendency to be backward. They were more likely to see religion and science as complementary and to view religiosity as a product of socialization and social pressure, and some also showed less motivation to eliminate all supernaturalism from society. They were, however, more likely than atheists in the Midwest to believe in passing laws that would create their ideal type of society.

These findings lend support to the contact hypothesis in that atheists' increased interaction and familiarity with those who were religious in the Bible Belt apparently diminished the atheists' fear of their desire and ability to politically dominate society. While they dislike some characteristics of believers, such as intolerance, they do not fear them or their efforts to take over society. The pervasive presence of religion in the Bible Belt apparently makes it more normative than in the Midwest. With increased contact and interaction with those who are religious, irrational fears and concerns are lessened.[26]

SUMMARY

In an attempt to piece together the observations of previous research, the curious history of atheism, our guiding questions and assumptions, and the findings from our analysis of the respondents in this study, we do find some expected patterns and a few non sequiturs in explaining the emergence of modern atheism—even modern atheistic fundamentalism.

Our respondents were, as previous studies have shown, in the social majority in terms of race, education, age, and income, regardless of where they lived. They were overwhelmingly white, well educated, older, and more affluent, all characteristics consistent with political conservatism, or so one would think. They were more likely to be social and political progressives with a strong allegiance to science. In a recent study of the politicization of science, trust in science has remained constant among Americans since the 1970s, with the exception of conservatives and those who frequently attend church.[27] These have had a diminishing trust in science and its capacity to reveal ultimate truth and to find answers for fundamental human problems.

The allegiance to and trust in science we observed among atheists seems to only be strengthening, while conservatives and those who are religious find that the end of science may be yet more science and the unintended consequences of scientific breakthroughs (such as the Internet and the proliferation of pornography) and that science may lead to what they see as erroneous conclusions about morality, political authority, the authority of the Bible, and the existence of God. We suspect that these conservative traditionalists are like the Ancients of the eighteenth-century Battle of the Books: at first enamored with the prospects of science but eventually experiencing disenchantment and an even stronger embracing of faith and tradition.

However, this simply may be an artifact in how trust in science is measured. A single measure of trust in the scientific community and those who run scientific agencies may give biased results. It may not be distrust in science at all, but a distrust of overly politicized scientific agencies and communities. This may be true for conservatives among whom a distrust of scientific institutions may indicate a skepticism toward government, not science. But for those who attend religious services regularly, we would still argue that, seeing that scientific findings tend to support more liberal agendas and demoralize issues that are viewed by the religious as inherently moral, science is not a potential source of truth.

This value-free ideal of amoral scientific fact is convenient for atheists, who tend not to believe in moral absolutes, as is the case with most progressives. Not that they believe in immorality. In chapter 6 we established atheists' beliefs in a humanistic version of morality not dependent on divine revelation. As was observed in chapter 5, active atheism with humanistic morality is married to political progressivism, and here we would add that active atheism with humanistic morality is also married to scientific empiricism, not just logic.

Science is part of a modernity that Peter Berger claims brought about reactionary new—or at least with a new emphasis—conservative beliefs and orientations.[28] Whereas modernity brings abstraction and an allegorical, critical way of studying scripture, religious fundamentalism responds with a renewed emphasis on scripture as revelation and literal truth. Absolute and definite answers based on a literal reading of scripture give conservative Christians some comfort, but it may be the implications of such literalism that has given rise to the apostasy of many modern nones.[29]

Biblical interpretation had, by the time of the rise of critical, scientific methods, already been affected by shifts in broader cultural practices for determining what was true and authoritative. There had been a shift to an emphasis on the certainty of knowledge and to a questioning of what was received or inherited as possibly unreliable or imprecise.[30] The influence of science also had an effect on the move toward precision of knowledge and suspicion of what was taken by faith. We can see these notions come alive in the words of our respondents who insist on empirical, precise, verifiable knowledge that God exists. If such evidence is not provided, there is no basis for assuming his existence or the authority of his alleged scriptures.

With modernity came an insistence that all discourse be held at the most precise and empirical level, which is scientific and follows scientific logic. For a time religion bought into this, its scholars wanting to support their beliefs in terms that were more acceptable to the broader world, which was more and more empirically oriented. With that came apologetics based on rational arguments for the existence of a supreme being (apologetics have been around for millennia, though in this age they were elevated to new heights of public discourse).

What we find as we study the explanations of our respondents is a rejection of religion's capacity to appeal to anything scientific. In fact, none of our respondents even mentioned that they had, in their search for truth (if they believed in such a thing), studied apologetic arguments or the defenses of religion that have been published by religious scholars. This may be because (1) they simply failed to mention it, (2) they simply chose not to explore religious alternatives and literature before obtaining an atheist identity, or (3) they simply believed apologetic arguments were not based on science and already had an overriding commitment to science as the only arbiter of ultimate truth. Virtually all atheists appeal, so it seems, to scientific, quantifiable data and not just logical statements.[31]

Going back to Duns Scotus, now it seems that it's irrelevant whether God is other or just more. Now the debate boils down to the rules of the game and the turf on which such an argument can be won or lost. While it seems that there is a historic dialectic between atheists and theists, today it seems that they are rattling swords on two different fields of battle. As we might say, they're not even in the same ballpark. Neither has the capacity to offer any evidence that the other sees as valuable.

In this public debate, it seems that religion, especially in its fundamentalist forms, explains the reaction formation of modern atheism, and the social values and voice of atheism explain how and why religion morphs as it does. Again, it is a dialectic of sorts, with no synthesis in sight.

As observed in chapter 5, there seem to be some inconsistencies in the political posturing of atheists and progressives versus theists and political conservatives. Whereas progressives, and thus atheists, tend to want political intervention when it seems that such intervention will further their own causes, they do not want government intervention when they perceive that such intrusion might interfere with individual rights. The government should legalize abortion with no restrictions and should not impose restrictions on behavior that is deemed immoral or unethical only by religious standards, such as same-sex marriage. But they welcome government intervention when it fits their political progressive vision. The government should raise taxes to take care of the poor and should fine those who violate environmental regulations. Atheists have a political vision of society that negates the political vision they see coming from conservative Christians, and this, rather than some overarching value, seems to motivate what they desire out of society.

With the current deadlock in government, the influence of the Tea Party in forcing conservatives to hold fast to their ideals, and an overall failure of the middle (where compromise has historically been the vehicle to move legislation through), it appears that Congress reflects a growing polarization of American society in terms of progressives and conservatives. In fact, earlier research found that although there does not seem to be a general polarization of American society, such polarization did seem to be taking place between Republican conservatives and Democratic progressives. [32]

This polarization possibly reflects a growing polarization between progressives and conservatives, or, in our instance, between atheists and theists and their political representatives. The language heats up, productivity fails, and again we find the representatives of these respective positions in different ballparks.

Whether the emphasis is on science or politics or any other area of life, it seems that atheists do what is quite predictable. They support efforts, public or private, that justify their belief systems and advance society in the direction they believe it should go, which is almost without exception in the way of progress. Old and outdated ways of thinking, often entrenched in religion, are just anchors that hold us back from that progress. Conservative theists do the same with opposing goals and rationalizations.

Chapter Eight

Summary and Conclusion

We began this look into atheism with some basic assumptions, and we have attempted to remain open and unbiased in case the findings failed to support our initial and rather informal hypotheses. As we followed and tested these assumptions, in many cases we found sound, supportive evidence in the words of atheists themselves. Placed in historical and cultural context, their arguments and sentiments made sense. In other cases, we discovered enlightening twists on those early assumptions, and in some cases we found little support at all.

OUR ASSUMPTIONS AND RATIONALE

After listing our basic assumptions, we want to systematically explore them in light of our participants' comments and the existing research to see if they find support. In the first chapter we made the following assumptions.

Our first and perhaps most basic assumption we borrowed from Gavin Hyman:[1] Atheism attempts to negate the messages and social action of religion. We tested this by reviewing the relationship between atheism and various theisms throughout history and by listening to our participants' comments in the context of broader social and religious beliefs and activities in modern American culture.

Following on the first assumption, we also went into this project with the expectation of finding parallels between the phenomenon of the new, aggressive expressions of atheism and the assertive, politically active movements in conservative Christianity. This apparent polarization and invigoration of both extremes may find its origin in the general influence of progressivism—especially its emphasis on science and humanism—on American culture, including religion.

Atheists may not understand morality as having a basis in divine revelation, but they clearly do have a strong sense of morality derived from ideas of social evolution and an allegiance to humanism. As some of their recent advertisements have stated, millions of people are good without God. The conflict with theists is not so much over morality itself but over the source of morality and the implications for social policy and law.

Central to the conflict between atheists and theists is the importance of power and control. This is clearly demonstrated in contemporary evidence that the struggle has spilled over into the realm of politics, the arena in which decisions are made regarding social boundaries and the establishment of social structure. As viewed by atheists and theists, this means the imposition of morality on many who may not share the same understanding of its basis. Atheists and theists have different ideas about morality and where those boundaries should be drawn, leading to conflict in the arena where those decisions are made—politics.

Finally, we attempted to test contact theory to discover if frequency and type of interaction with believers had any influence on the attitudes of atheists. By selecting some respondents from a liberal, Midwestern region of the country and others from the Bible Belt, we wanted to see if those differing geographic locations had regional effects on atheists.

ATHEISM AS THE NEGATION OF RELIGION AND RELIGIOUS INFLUENCE

By definition, an atheist is someone who does not believe in a God, and most usually someone who does not believe in gods or a supernatural world at all. If it were all that simple, we should wonder why there has been such a historic battle between believers and nonbelievers. Why not allow people to believe whatever they wish? Why the need for conflict? If you believe in someone who is invisible, while I hold that if that someone is not empirically verifiable, then he or she is not believable, why must the result be conflict between us?

The historic fact is that it is not that simple. Religion has always been a powerful force, forming ethnic and national identities, justifying conquest and war, shaping civil law and morality, demonizing the enemy, and drawing social boundaries that define who is in and who is out.[2] It has been used as a litmus test for fidelity and as a rationalization for genocide and suicide bombings. Religious rationalizations appeal to ultimate authority and so take on an extraordinary mantle of power against which no mere human can stand.

As long as there have been religious explanations for social order, there have been those who, in opposition to that order, have at the same time opposed its religious foundations. Greeks and Romans found opposition from Jews and Christians, their conflict at times described as basically religious. But even a cursory reading of their histories reveals those conflicts as an opposition to imperialism by minorities who rejected the authority of the state. Theistic rationalizations were central to Greek and Roman conquests, and those who opposed their conquest were labeled atheists, or those who opposed the authority of the state. Atheism in that era was technically not godlessness; it was a label attached to anyone who did not vow allegiance to the gods of the state. The Jews and Christians clearly were believers, but they opposed the gods of the Greeks and Romans.

In more recent history we find the full development of a materialist atheism, which already had roots among ancient Greek philosophers. With the growth of science as *the* way of knowing, and the emancipating ideas of French social philosophers, atheism developed as a political force that opposed the religious and political dominance of the Roman Catholic Church and, in particular, the French elitist state. The arguments of these atheists and philosophers were not so much theological as they were accusatory of the abuses of church and state, and they appealed to reason and science as the basis for ordering society. As others have said, there was a world-changing shift from *rex lex* (the king is law) to *lex rex* (rationally derived law should be the supreme authority). Atheism brought with it a delegitimation of rule by divine right and a shift to reason and science. At the same time it became a means of self-identification rather than an accusation.

Although this major shift in the alliance between church and state and the ideal of rationality as the basis of authority had tremendous impact on European societies, early American settlers adapted rational, democratic ideas to a common Protestantism. In its earliest American form, that was pluralism. With immigration of Catholic and Jewish populations, the United States was challenged to redefine pluralism, and it eventually adopted a Judeo-Christian ethic as a moral guide. Americans were distrustful of those from parts of that broad tradition other than their own, but atheism as true godlessness was, by all accounts, extremely rare.

It was not until the mid-nineteenth century, with the influence of ideas from people such as Darwin, Huxley, and Mill, that atheism began to find footing and a voice in American society. While self-identified atheists were primarily found among academics and intellectuals, their ideas trickled down to seminaries and into the pulpits of America's churches. From that time there has been a cleaving of American religion into progressive religion, which adapts science and reason to religious ethics, and conservative or traditional religion, which clings to scriptural literalism and, as some of our respondents pointed out, an anti-science bias.

AGGRESSIVE ATHEISM AS A RESPONSE TO CONSERVATIVE CHRISTIAN POLITICAL ACTION

Contemporary atheism, particularly the new, aggressive, fundamentalist atheism, is overtly anti-religious. The respondents in our survey and interviews support the popular atheist literature in their allegiance to science, while accusing the religious of being backward, anti-scientific, at times sexist, and even delusional.

The aggressive nature of contemporary atheism appears to have its roots in the fundamentalist reaction to the progressive movement in the late nineteenth and early twentieth centuries, and the conservative social and political actions of those who moved to the Religious Right in response to progressivism's infiltration of religion. For the most part, atheists seem only slightly annoyed by those who hold to traditional religious beliefs. But when religious conservatives take political action in order to impose policy and law on a society that they see as drifting toward progressive ideology and moral relativism, atheists take action. For this reason, we found it difficult to separate the missions of organizations that were clearly promoting atheism and those that were advocating the separation of church and state.

In summary, our research led us to support the argument that atheism seeks to negate religion, especially religion that attempts to control social and moral boundaries through political action. We also believe that the opposite can be argued—that religious beliefs and activities tend to be formed in response to their opposition (in this case, progressive and atheistic beliefs and activities). For example, it is clear that the early twentieth-century Christian fundamentalist movement was rooted in the perceived threat of Darwinism and progressive social ideas. Atheism and conservative theism appear to form themselves and their actions in response to the positions, voices, and political actions of the other.

ATHEISTIC AND CHRISTIAN MORALITIES: DIFFERING BASES FOR ORDERING SOCIETY

According to some conservative believers, atheists have no basis for morality and are in general immoral, amoral, or borrowers from Western notions of morality that are based on Judeo-Christianity. Without divine direction and moral boundaries for ordering human behavior, they say, how can there be any true basis for establishing morality? For some conservative believers, the moral relativism that certainly must emerge from atheistic camps is no morality at all. Of course, variations in the definition of morality within the Christian world, particularly between progressives and conservatives, leave that world open to criticism that even with a divinely ordered morality, in practice Christian morality is relative as well.

We find in our study a very strong sense of morality among atheists, although clearly not a morality with the same divine mandate as Christian morality. The morality of atheism appears to emerge from atheists' allegiance to progressive ideals and to science. Whatever facilitates social progress and is rational is moral. For example, sound scientific education of children equips them to assist in social progress. Whatever impedes social progress is immoral, including the exercise of religion and the socialization or "brainwashing" of children into religious worldviews that atheists see as promoting distorted ideologies and attachments to irrational superstition. Not only does this impede social progress, but it also brings with it social toxins such as sexism, racism, and homophobia.

We also found a link between atheist morality and an atheistic notion of soteriology, or salvation. What is good is what saves us. Conservative Christians believe that humans are saved from eternal damnation by the sacrifice and saving grace of Jesus of Nazareth.[3] Depending on the tradition, the conditions of that salvation are also tied to moral behavior. If you believe, and if you behave in moral ways in line with Christian ideas of morality, then you will be saved. That is clearly no comfort to atheists. Although they do not believe in either eternal damnation or the saving grace of Jesus, they do have a sense that society is headed somewhere, and what helps in that progress toward human and social potential is good. Atheists tend to tie morality to salvation, though the terms are obviously not used as conservative Christians would use them.

Many atheists in our study also expressed a strong belief in humanism, a philosophical approach that views humanity as essentially good, worthy of dignity, and capable of fulfilling its potential through reason. What is good is what helps humans fulfill their potential and maintain their dignity. Perhaps for this reason, atheists and progressives in general support the dignity and rights of all who are socially marginalized, including immigrants, women, those whose sexual preferences differ from traditional heterosexuality, and racial or ethnic minorities. We heard no defense for the basis of this humanism other than the argument that it is consistent with social progress. It is also possible that the answer may be found in sociobiology, a form of social evolutionism. What is good is what has survived, including forms of social relationships, behaviors, and organizations. Whatever the genesis of this idea, it is common among atheists and foundational for their sense of morality as well as for their outrage at the abuses of religion that have marginalized people and robbed them of their inherent dignity.

THE ROOT OF THE PROBLEM: POWER AND CONTROL

In our previous discussion of atheism's attempts to negate the influence of religion, we addressed the central issue that we confront here. Scratch the surface of most conflicts, religious or not, and you will find people and parties contending for valuable resources. That is one of the foundational principles of conflict theory in the social sciences, and one that we believe targets the central issue of the debate between theists and atheists.

What is it that each wants? What valuable resources are so precious that they inspire dismissal of others' ideas, dehumanization of fellow humans, harsh political battles, and even violence? In most cases the contested resources have very little to do with theology or even belief and disbelief. Even in inter-religious conflicts such as the ongoing struggle between the Israelis and Palestinians, or in intra-religious conflicts such as what we find in Northern Ireland, seldom are the real issues religious. Religious labels are given to contests over land, physical resources, and forms of authority. A political struggle over a relatively small corner of the Emerald Isle is publicized as a struggle between Irish Catholics and Protestants (or Anglo-Catholics) who are loyal to the British throne. Even the Thirty Years' War that followed the Protestant Reformation was at least as much based on regional control of land as it was on the split between Catholics and Protestants.

And there is little that is inherently incendiary between Israeli Jews and Palestinians, whether Christian or Muslim. However, place them together on land that is sacred to both traditions, with one exercising political and even physical and economic control of the other, and conflict erupts. Rather than cousins, they become enemies. As enemies in an eternal struggle, how do they ensure a future generation that supports their position? Education and early socialization. Loyalty and ideology are propagated in schools, mosques, synagogues, and around dinner tables, as are visions of the demonized enemy. Allies are recruited from outside, and so we see an international division between backers of the State of Israel and backers of the Palestinian cause.

The conflict between atheists and theists has clear parallels. As long as one side is not threatening the other, as long as the main issue is belief or nonbelief, conflict has been the exception, not the rule. However, as progressivism in the forms of evolutionary theory, materialism, and humanism began to impact American intellectuals, seminaries, and clergy, conservative Christians felt that the moral fabric of society was threatened and began assertive responses in the early twentieth century. Those assertive responses came in two very visible ways: through political action and through influence of public school curricula. In order to preserve traditional order and morality, conservative theists wanted to ensure that their values and beliefs were supported in public schools. And in order to ensure continued social progress, atheists and other progressives wanted science and rationality taught in public schools. Both theists and atheists pay taxes to support public schools, and both expect their values to be upheld. Theists who started religious schools fought for vouchers to recover their tax contributions so they could send their children to religious schools, an effort that met with strong opposition from progressives. Others began to home-school, a movement that has picked up momentum as progressive values have become the norm in American public schools.

CONTACT HYPOTHESIS: DOES FREQUENT INTERACTION WITH CONSERVATIVE CHRISTIANS AFFECT THE ATTITUDES AND OPINIONS OF ATHEISTS?

Support for contact hypothesis regarding such issues as racial attitudes has been found, although not always in expected ways or directions.[4] It is an idea that is intuitively appealing—that familiarity with those who are different affects one's attitudes toward them. In the case of atheists and theists, we made this assumption but were not clear on the direction of its impact. It is possible that familiarity and contact might cause Bible Belt atheists to have stronger personal, visceral reactions to conservative Christians or evangelicals. Conversely, actually knowing, working with, or attending class with conservative Christians and evangelicals might humanize them and reduce fears that they were engaged in a conspiracy to impose a Christian theocracy in the United States.

Our findings were mixed, but primarily we found support for the latter. Atheists from the Bible Belt were less concerned about a Christian theocracy or a Christian conspiracy than were their counterparts in the Midwest. Familiarity, in this case, seems to have humanized conservative Christians and mitigated fears that they were attempting to impose control or convert everyone. Bible Belt atheists did not care for Christian intolerance of others or their backward approach to science and notions of progress, although they were more likely than Midwestern atheists to entertain the possibility that science and religion might be complementary and even the possibility of a supernatural.

Contrary to earlier[5] findings that few atheists are apostates from religious backgrounds, we found that a number of atheists from the Bible Belt had grown up religious and apostatized to atheism rather than switching to another Christian denomination or becoming agnostic. Neither that study nor ours offer any empirical evidence to demonstrate the frequency of such apostasies, nor can we determine whether the recent rise in the number of those who self-identify as atheist is due to an actual increase in their numbers or rather to an increase in atheists who are willing to be public about that self-identification. Clearly more research is needed to answer that question.

UNDERSTANDING ATHEISM: WHERE DO WE GO FROM HERE?

In the following pages we would like to outline some of the issues that remain unresolved in research into atheism and progressivism in general. Our intent is to bring into the discussion some underlying issues that have not been fully addressed and to propose a research agenda for those who wish to contribute further to the literature on atheism and progressivism.

The philosophical difference of epistemology between atheists and theists seems to be the most intractable problem in resolving their conflict or at least bringing them into dialogue. At this point we will not even propose the possibility of full resolution; instead, we will suggest that a more peaceful coexistence may be found.

Most simply stated, do we understand morality as rules and boundaries revealed by a divine authority, or do we understand them as a rational assessment of the material world and the history of human evolution? Are they a divine or human creation? Or are they of divine origin yet subject to adaptation by rational humans as our species evolves over time and changes definitions to suit the culture and the spirit of the day? The first option is the approach of religious conservatives who contend that morality is divinely revealed and absolute, not adaptive to time, place, or culture. The second is a position held by atheists and humanists who dismiss any divine intervention and believe morality is a human construct that progresses over time. And the third option describes the basic approach of progressive religious groups: God exists and has influenced general moral principles over time, although biblical accounts are intended to be read as history and literature and are subject to the same foibles as any other literature. As we become enlightened, we should adapt previously accepted definitions and moral absolutes. For example, we in the West have become enlightened to the point that we now unequivocally define human slavery as wrong, even though the Bible does not.

The logic of Christian conservatives is the least adaptable. As an infamous (at least among progressives) bumper sticker says, "The Bible Says It. I Believe It. That Settles It." There is no room for negotiation. More moderate yet still relatively conservative Christians at least are able to debate the issues, typically using apologetics and historical arguments based on those of such figures as Thomas Aquinas. But their arguments seldom have much of an impact on atheists, who typically insist on empirical, scientific evidence for the existence of God, not theological or philosophical arguments.

Atheists likely will never be satisfied as long as they demand scientific evidence. In that case, about the best we can expect is for them to agree to disagree. And we cannot even expect that as long as either side is attempting to influence political processes in their favor. Nor will conservative Christians often be swayed by scientific evidence that the animal species of this world, including humans, evolved over extraordinary lengths of time. Many fundamentalist Christians and Orthodox Jews have in common the belief that the cosmos was created in six days and that human history spans 5,772 years. That time span is known because it was divinely revealed according to religious conservatives, a belief that scientifically oriented atheists and theists consider nonsense. To them, religious conservatives must be humming with their hands over their ears to avoid the obvious scientific evidence that contradicts such a timeline.

This problem of knowing, of how humans determine what is known and knowable, and of how it becomes known or knowable, has been a shadow issue in the whole history of atheism and theism. From its earliest days, Christian orthodoxy has confronted the heresy of gnosticism, which, among other things, proposed that salvation comes with the acquisition of esoteric, mystical truth that saves one from the evils of the material world. In this case, knowledge was exclusive and not available to the masses.

At the other end of this spectrum of certainty are atheists who propose that there absolutely is no God or supernatural. It is a firm disbelief. From gnosticism to atheism we have gone from exclusive, esoteric spiritual belief that regards the material world as evil to atheism that dismisses religious knowledge, esoteric or not, and embraces the physical world and the rational application of science as the means of knowing and ordering human society. Both are absolute in their confidence in their own epistemology.

In the middle of this continuum are two other options. One is agnosticism, which comes from the same root as "gnosticism," which means "knowledge." Agnosticism is basically the position that the existence of God and the supernatural are unknowable. For agnostics, even science is incapable of proving that God does not exist, and the best Christian apologetics cannot prove that God does exist. The one remaining option in this continuum is belief, or the camp of those who positively believe in the existence of God, believe that such knowledge is not exclusive or mystical, and believe that the physical world is a good gift given to humans for us to inhabit. However, knowledge by faith, a central tenet of conservative Christianity, is meaningless to scientific atheists.

Another issue in the atheism-theism debate is the question of whether, as the emerging United States found a way to forge a common Protestantism and eventually accepted a pluralism that included Catholics and Jews and ultimately the beliefs of people from the corners of the earth, a new common ethic is possible. Is there a common ethic under which we can at least find a tolerable pluralism?

In today's political and religious climate, such a common ethic and broad pluralism does not seem likely, except in the political and religious middle where extremism and fundamentalism do not make immediate enemies of others who hold dissimilar views. It is in the middle where there is likely more contact between believers and nonbelievers, and possibly less belief in the other's conspiracies and attempts to control. At the extremes, however, we see little movement. We do not expect members of the Tea Party movement in American politics to be very interested in forming coalitions with those who are economically and socially progressive. And we do not expect any rapprochement between assertive atheists and fundamentalist or even conservative Christians.

Other questions that need answers are exactly how many atheists there are in the United States, whether they actually are growing in number, and why there seems to be so much variation in these numbers from one study to the next. As presented in the first chapter, the Pew Forum on Religion & Public Life[6] found that only 5 percent of Americans did not believe in God or a universal spirit, and of that 5 percent only 24 percent self-identified as atheists. If we consider only those who self-label as actually being atheists, we are down to barely more than 1 percent of the American population.

Neither in our research nor in any other that we know of have investigators and interviewers been adequately sensitive to these discrepancies between beliefs and self-labels. In our approach, particularly with those in the face-to-face interviews, the sample was biased in that we asked for self-identified atheists to participate. We recruited them, thus excluding people who do not believe in God yet are not willing to self-identify as atheists. Is there a progression from one to the other? Is there a qualitative difference in what they actually believe or disbelieve? Are those who do not believe yet do not self-identify as atheists politically active, and do they affect political processes and public discourse in ways similar to self-identified atheists?

We also have identified the problem of the various routes that people take to atheism. Already well documented is the increase in religious switching among American Christians. We propose that some of the same broad social influences that contributed to a rise in religious switching may also have influenced individuals' willingness to transfer to nonreligious affiliations. When people leave religious affiliation, where do they go? Among those who become atheists, how many were at one time religious, and why did they decide to become atheists? And why, as we found, would atheists be more likely to have had religious backgrounds if they grew up and lived in the Bible Belt? Bob Altemeyer and Bruce Hunsberger[7] began to address this question with a series of case studies of those who had either converted or deconverted, but a more quantitative and representative approach might give us a better idea as to the broader patterns of apostasy in American society.

CONCLUSION

The most recent conflicts we have observed between believers and nonbelievers are, in our opinion, simply the latest incarnation of a very old debate between those who appeal to a supernatural authority and those who prefer to rely on human reason and observation. We purposely point out that it is authority that is the main sticking point, and where is authority exercised more powerfully than in politics? There are innumerable differences among Americans regarding a whole host of definitions, meanings, and subjective assessments of every facet of social life, and for the most part we simply observe the differences and agree to disagree, or we make allowances for cultural diversity. But it is when those ideas become ideologies that drive political processes that opponents take notice and respond.

One thing that atheists and theists in the West have in common is a linear concept of time: that our histories are important for shaping our ideas and identities and that our vision of the future shapes our social and political activity. The problem is that these two camps have entirely different ideas about what that future will be. Conservative believers live under the conviction that we must rely on divinely revealed truth to fight the good fight and ultimately win salvation in another world, or at least in a completely renewed one. Atheists believe the future is what we make of it through rational and scientific choices. To many conservative believers, the atheists' view leads to a moral relativism that renders humans incapable of fighting the good fight and receiving the heavenly reward. Most atheists believe that clinging to chimera and myth while denying scientific evidence is the antithesis of progress.

Each camp has a type of morality based on behavior that leads to the best possible outcome as the future unfolds. The conflict is made manifest when the two begin to engage in politics in order to impose morality and structure on an entire society, including those who disagree with the source of authority behind that morality and structure. Determining what the outcome of those political struggles will be is, even with the best social research, a guessing game. What is evident to us is that little progress will be made in resolving this conflict as long as the dialogue is relegated to those at the extremes. Answers are most likely to come from those in the middle, those who are familiar with others with whom they disagree but are willing to know them and work with them and respect them despite their differences.

Appendix 1

Open-Ended Questions Used in Online Survey

1. How would you define the Christian Right?
2. Please describe your general attitude toward the Christian Right.
3. Is there any specific characteristic of members of the Christian Right or political issue that they support that drives this attitude?
4. What is the most positive thing you can say about the Christian Right?
5. What is the most negative thing you can say about the Christian Right?
6. What is your most memorable personal encounter with a member of the Christian Right? What happened in that encounter and how did you feel about that experience? Please list more than one such encounter if you so desire.
7. Did that encounter alter how you perceived members of the Christian Right? If so, then how did it do that?
8. Imagine that you can choose who is going to be your neighbor. Please rate the desirability of having one of the following individuals as your neighbor:

   A vocal Republican who is not a Christian.
   A vocal Christian who is apolitical.

9. Which of the two hypothetical neighbors do you desire less and why do you have a lower desire for the neighbor you ranked lower?
10. Would it bother you if most of your neighbors were members of the Christian Right, and if so, then why?
11. Do you think that we should pass laws that would affect members of the Christian Right? If you do want to pass such law(s), what would they be and why?

12. Are there any comments about the Christian Right you would like to add that you did not get a chance to in any of the other questions?

Appendix 2

Interview Schedule for Atheists

1. Tell me about your background. Where did you grow up?
2. Describe the atmosphere of your family as you were growing up. Were your parents religious? Were your parents restrictive because of their religion?
3. Did you have a lot of religious friends as you were growing up? (Probe: What sort of religion did they practice?)
4. Tell me about how you thought about religion as you grew up.
5. How would you define what an atheist is?
6. How old were you when you became an atheist? (Probe: What did you believe before becoming an atheist? If from birth, then skip question 7.)
7. Who was the most influential person in helping you to come to that decision? (Probe: Why?)
8. What was happening in your life when you became an atheist? (Probe to find out the social influences that affected this decision.)
9. What is the most powerful logical argument that convinced you about atheism?
10. Since your becoming an atheist, has there ever been a time when you have had any doubts about atheism? (Probe: If yes, then what caused those doubts?)
11. Have your personal atheistic beliefs helped you through troubled times? (Probe: Has it added to joyous times?)
12. Why do you think that people continue to believe in the supernatural?
13. What objections or concerns do you have about the way religion is practiced today?

14. What would your ideal society look like, particularly as it concerns the prevalence of religion? (Probe: What are you willing to do to create such a society?)

Notes

1. UNDERSTANDING ATHEISM IN THE UNITED STATES

1. Gavin Hyman, "Atheism in Modern History," in *The Cambridge Companion to Atheism*, ed. Michael Martin (Cambridge: Cambridge University Press, 2007).

2. Christopher Hitchens, *God Is Not Great: How Religion Poisons Everything* (New York: Twelve Hatchette Book Group, 2007).

3. Richard Dawkins, *The God Delusion* (Boston: Mariner Books, 2006).

4. Victor J. Stenger, *The New Atheism: Taking a Stand for Science and Reason* (Amherst, NY: Prometheus Books, 2009).

5. Dan Barker, *Godless: How an Evangelical Preacher Became One of America's Leading Atheists* (Berkeley, CA: Ulysses Press, 2008).

6. Jeff Nall, "Fundamentalist Atheism and Its Intellectual Failures," *Humanity and Society* 32 (August 2008).

7. Michael Martin, *Atheism: A Philosophical Justification* (Philadelphia, PA: Temple University Press, 1990).

8. The emphasis here is not the extent to which one does not believe in God, but the extent to which one believes in and expresses arguments against the existence of God. Either way, this fits with Martin's (*Atheism*, 1990) definition of "positive atheists."

9. www.atheists.org.

10. Miguel Farias and Mansur Lalljee, "Holistic Individualism in the Age of Aquarius: Measuring Individualism/Collectivism in New Age, Catholic, and Atheist/Agnostic Groups," *Journal for the Scientific Study of Religion* 47, no. 2 (2008), compared New Age, Catholic, and atheist/agnostic groups and found that atheists and agnostics were more likely than the other groups to have a physical understanding of themselves.

11. Pew Forum on Religion & Public Life, "Not All Nonbelievers Call Themselves Atheists," www.pewforum.org.

12. Barry A. Kosmin and Ariela Keysar, *American Religious Identification Survey: Summary Report* (Hartford, CT: Trinity College, 2009).

13. Darren E. Sherkat, "Beyond Belief: Atheism, Agnosticism, and Theistic Certainty in the United States," *Sociological Spectrum* 28 (2008).

14. Phil Zuckerman, "Atheism: Contemporary Numbers and Patterns," in *The Cambridge Companion to Atheism*, ed. Michael Martin (Cambridge: Cambridge University Press, 2007).

15. This also could be explained in the same way: At times, "epidemics" in the United States are observed, but testing and reporting have improved so greatly that the actual incidence and prevalence of disease have changed little. It could be that atheists are coming out, growing in

their comfort with the label, and becoming more courageous in their self-identification as atheists, so there is an appearance of growth as an artifact of social change regarding the inclusion of all marginalized populations.

16. Nall, "Fundamentalist Atheism," 264.

17. Michael Lienesch, *In the Beginning: Fundamentalism, the Scopes Trial, and the Making of the Antievolution Movement* (Chapel Hill: University of North Carolina Press, 2007).

18. By "mainstream Christianity," we mean the original institutions of the most prominent denominations in the United States that have tended to become more progressive over the last century, with perhaps the exclusion of Baptists. Mainstream denominations include, for example, the Episcopal Church in the United States of America (ECUSA) and the Presbyterian Church, U.S.A. (PCUSA). Most mainstream denominations have declined in numbers, although many of their evangelical offshoots, such as the Presbyterian Church of America (PCA), have grown dramatically.

19. Kosmin and Keysar, *American Religious Identification Survey*, 5.

20. Dean M. Kelley, *Why Conservative Churches Are Growing: A Study in Sociology* (New York: Harper & Row, 1972).

21. Paul DiMaggio, John Evans, and Bethany Bryson, "Have Americans' Social Attitudes Become More Polarized?" *American Journal of Sociology* 102, no. 3 (1996).

22. We do not mean to say that these battles have been won—that African Americans do not continue to experience discrimination, that women don't see their opportunities limited, and that atheists do not know that a majority of Americans do not trust them because of their unbelief. What these groups have in common is a sense that history is on their side and the shared courage to stand up and, unapologetically, announce themselves and their rights.

23. Penny Edgell, Joseph Gerteis, and Douglas Hartmann, "Atheists as 'Other': Moral Boundaries and Cultural Membership in American Society," *American Sociological Review* 71, no. 2 (2006).

24. Caydee Ensey, "Students Attend Inaugural Reason Rally," *North Texas Daily*, March 27, 2012.

25. Hitchens, *God Is Not Great*.

26. Irving M. Zeitlin, *The Religious Experience: Classical Philosophical and Social Theories* (Upper Saddle River, NJ: Pearson Press, 2004).

27. Jan N. Bremmer, "Atheism in Antiquity," in *The Cambridge Companion to Atheism*, ed. Michael Martin (Cambridge: Cambridge University Press, 2007).

28. Ibid., 20–21. In Eusebius, *The Ecclesiastical History of Eusebius Pamphilus*, trans. Christian Frederick Cruse (Grand Rapids, MI: Baker Book House, 1955), written in the late third and/or the early fourth century CE, Polycarp is quoted as saying, "Away with the impious" (146). Certainly he was aware that his Roman accusers maintained a form of pantheism or polytheism, so he was not using terminology intended to mean they had no religion. He was clearly and derisively accusing them of impiety toward his own form of monotheism. Prior to this moment he had welcomed the guards who had come to arrest him, sat them down to a dinner, and requested that they "partake of food largely" (145), during which time he said his last prayers. It was the accusation that such a godly elder of the church be accused of atheism that finally brought such contempt that he felt compelled to offer his own accusation.

29. Hyman, "Atheism in Modern History," 29.

30. James Thrower, *Western Atheism: A Short History* (Amherst, NY: Prometheus, Books, 2000).

31. James A. Haught, *2000 Years of Disbelief: Famous People with the Courage to Doubt* (Amherst, NY: Prometheus Books, 1996).

32. Jennifer Michael Hecht, *Doubt: A History* (New York: Harper, 2006).

33. Hyman, "Atheism in Modern History," 29.

34. Ibid., 37.

35. Ian Barbour, *Religion and Science: Historical and Contemporary Issues* (San Francisco: HarperSanFrancisco, 1997); Philip Clayton, *God and Contemporary Science* (Grand Rapids, MI: Wm. B. Eerdmans, 1997); Hugh Ross, *The Creator and the Cosmos: How the Greatest Scientific Discoveries of the Century Reveal God* (Colorado Springs, CO: NavPress, 1993).

36. John Polkinghorne, *Belief in God in an Age of Science* (New Haven, CT: Yale University Press, 2003).

37. Peter L. Berger, *Pyramids of Sacrifice: Political Ethics and Social Change* (Garden City, NY: Anchor Books, 1976).

38. Jack P. Gibbs, *Control: Sociology's Central Notion* (Urbana: University of Illinois Press, 1989).

39. Max Weber, *The Theory of Social and Economic Organization* (New York: Oxford University Press, 1947).

40. We acknowledge that other traditions emerged that were more Dionysian or ordered from shared feeling, spontaneity, and direct revelation from God or other sources of authority that cannot be labeled as purely rational. But the beginning of the Reformation movement was rational, and primarily based in biblical study and not on tradition.

41. Matthew T. Loveland, "Religious Switching: Preference Development, Maintenance, and Change," *Journal for the Scientific Study of Religion* 42, no. 1 (2003); C. Kirk Hadaway, "Denominational Switching and Religiosity," *Review of Religious Research* 21, no. 4 (1980); Dean R. Hoge, Benton Johnson, and Donald Al Luidens, "Types of Denominational Switching among Protestant Young Adults," *Journal for the Scientific Study of Religion* 34, no. 2 (1995).

42. An example of this questioning of authority, or the limitation of authority's capacity to regulate belief and behavior, can be found in the recent debate about President Obama's attempt to mandate that all health care institutions provide contraception and women's health services that are objectionable to Roman Catholics. In April of 2011 a study conducted by the Guttmacher Institute—Rachel K. Jones and Joerg Dreweke, *Countering Conventional Wisdom: New Evidence on Religion and Contraceptive Use* (New York: Guttmacher Institute, 2011)—used a nationally representative sample, and reported that Catholic women used contraceptives in forms and at rates comparable to women in other religious groups.

43. John G. Jackson, "Hubert Henry Harrison: The Black Socrates," American Atheists, http://atheists.org/content/hubert-henry-harrison-black-socrates.

44. Berger, *Pyramids of Sacrifice*, 1–4.

45. Stephen L. Carter, *The Culture of Disbelief: How American Law and Politics Trivialize Religious Devotion* (New York: Basic Books, 1993).

46. Lienesch, *In the Beginning*; Ronald Numbers, *Darwinism Comes to America* (Cambridge, MA: Harvard University Press, 1998).

47. Traditionally the term "eternal damnation" has been interpreted to mean damnation and suffering that lasts forever. However, some, such as Edward William Fudge in *The Fire That Consumes: A Biblical and Historical Study of the Doctrine of Final Punishment* (Lincoln, NE: iUniverse.com, 2001), have argued that eternal should be interpreted as "final," or a damnation that cannot be revoked. In the latter, the damned individual does not suffer forever, but the death they experience is the final termination of their life. They are not granted immortality and therefore are mortal, or subject to death. Atheists point out the highly motivating dimension of the former definition and thus the church's preference for the interpretation that the suffering will last forever.

48. George Yancey, *Interracial Contact and Social Change* (Boulder, CO: Lynne Rienner, 2007).

2. A BRIEF HISTORY OF ATHEISM

1. For more complete histories, we refer the reader to James Thrower, *Western Atheism: A Short History* (Amherst, NY: Prometheus Books, 2000), and Michael Martin, ed., *The Cambridge Companion to Atheism* (Cambridge: Cambridge University Press, 2007), both excellent and reliable sources on the history of atheism.

2. Gavin Hyman, "Atheism in Modern History," in *The Cambridge Companion to Atheism*, ed. Michael Martin (Cambridge: Cambridge University Press, 2007).

3. Depending on the group under consideration, Christian groups are divided on this just as they are on moral issues such as abortion and gay marriage. But even conservative Christians

tend now to favor inclusion as an ideal for minorities and equal rights for women. The general assumption in contemporary American culture is inclusion.

4. Jan N. Bremmer, "Atheism in Antiquity," in *The Cambridge Companion to Atheism*, ed. Michael Martin (Cambridge: Cambridge University Press, 2007).

5. All scriptural references come from *The New Oxford Annotated Bible*, New Revised Standard Version (New York: Oxford University Press, 1991).

6. Hyman, "Atheism in Modern History"; Gavin Hyman, *A Short History of Atheism* (London: I.B. Tauris, 2010).

7. Bremmer, "Atheism in Antiquity," 15.

8. Ibid., 16.

9. Because the focus of this work is on atheists, we limit the discussion to their characteristics and behaviors. Of course, it is equally true that the religious have historically denigrated the irreligious, going so far at times as to murder them. Those who take this conflict seriously and have given themselves to it understand the intensity of the conflict and what is at stake.

10. www.chabad.org.

11. *The New Oxford Annotated Bible*, New Revised Standard Version (New York: Oxford University Press, 1991).

12. Hyman, "Atheism in Modern History," 37.

13. Information on Duns Scotus was taken from http://plato.stanford.edu/entries/duns-scotus.

14. His actual name was John Duns. He hailed from Scotland and is typically referred to as Duns Scotus.

15. Hyman, "Atheism in Modern History," 39.

16. Ian Barbour, *Religion and Science: Historical and Contemporary Issues* (San Francisco: HarperSanFrancisco, 1997).

17. Christopher Hitchens, *God Is Not Great: How Religion Poisons Everything* (New York: Twelve Hatchette Book Group, 2007).

18. Peter L. Berger, *A Far Glory: The Quest for Faith in an Age of Credulity* (New York: Free Press, 1992).

19. Joan DeJean, *Ancients against Moderns: Culture Wars and Making of a Fin De Siècle* (Chicago: University of Chicago Press, 1997).

20. Thrower, *Western Atheism*, 97.

21. Hyman, "Atheism in Modern History," 30.

22. Ibid., 33.

23. Ibid., 35.

24. Irving M. Zeitlin, *The Religious Experience: Classical Philosophical and Social Theories* (Upper Saddle River, NJ: Pearson Press, 2004), ix.

25. Hyman, "Atheism in Modern History," 30.

26. Thrower, *Western Atheism*, 129.

27. James Hunter, *Culture Wars: The Struggle to Define America* (New York: Basic Books, 1991), 69.

28. Ronald Numbers, *Darwinism Comes to America* (Cambridge, MA: Harvard University Press, 1998), 62.

29. Rodney Stark and Roger Finke, *Acts of Faith: Explaining the Human Side of Religion* (Berkeley: University of California Press, 2000).

30. Hyman, *A Short History of Atheism*, 9.

31. Max Weber, *The Protestant Ethic and the Spirit of Capitalism* (London: Unwin Paperbacks, 1930/1985); Richard Hofstadter, *Anti-Intellectualism in American Life* (New York: Vintage, 1963).

32. Hofstadter, *Anti-Intellectualism in American Life*, 80.

33. Numbers, *Darwinism Comes to America*.

34. www.aclu.org/aclu-history.

35. www.aclu.org/aclu-history.

36. www.atheists.org.

37. www.ffrf.org/about/year-in-review.

38. www.pfaw.org/about-us/our-mission-and-vision.

3. WHO ARE THE ATHEISTS?

1. Barry A. Kosmin and Ariela Keysar, *American Religious Identification Survey* (Hartford, CT: Trinity College, 2009).

2. We define cultural progressives as individuals who either support the progressive position on important cultural political issues, such as abortion and homosexuality, or oppose the interference of traditional religionists who may impose a more conservative perspective on such issues. Such individuals do not need to be atheists; however, clearly atheists are more likely to be cultural progressives than non-atheists since they do not have religious influences that compel them to accept a more traditionalist perspective on cultural issues.

3. There is an exception to this tendency. We found that some individuals connected to the Christian Right joined these oppositional organizations in an effort to monitor them. We eliminated several of our surveys when it was clear that the individuals filling out the survey were quite sympathetic to the Christian Right. It is possible that a couple of these "plants" got through our screens; however, one or two individuals are unlikely to skew our results.

4. Although the writers of letters to the editor are not necessarily official leaders in the atheist social movement, we contend that the leaders of these movements act as gatekeepers in which letters will be featured in the literature. Therefore, although they did not write the letters themselves, we believe that the letters are highly likely to reflect the attitudes of the atheist leaders.

5. George Yancey, "Who Has Religious Prejudice? Differing Sources of Anti-Religious Animosity in the United States," *Review of Religious Research* 52, no. 2 (2010).

6. For secondary literature, see Bob Altemeyer and Bruce Hunsberger, *Amazing Conversions: Why Some Turn to Faith and Others Abandon Religion* (Amherst, NY: Prometheus Books, 1997); Satoshi Kanazawa, "Why Liberals and Atheists Are More Intelligent," *Social Psychology Quarterly* 73, no. 1 (2010); Richard Lynn, John Harvey, and Helmuth Nyborg, "Average Intelligence Predicts Atheism Rates across 137 Nations," *Intelligence* 37, no. 1 (2009).

7. There is also a potential difference because of the mode of communication. There is evidence that because of the secrecy of the Internet, individuals are more rude when they provide online responses than when they are face to face with an interviewer. Our observation is that interview respondents were less likely to use bombastic and demonizing language than our online respondents. Online responses may allow an individual to feel freer to show emotions that are not seen as acceptable in polite company.

8. Naturally we have kept copies of these statements and can produce them if there is question about the accuracy of their citation. But given that we generally use them to show support for concepts illustrated in our online survey and interviews instead of using them to introduce new concepts, there is questionable value in challenging the authenticity of these quotes.

9. Because we obtained our atheists from connections to official organizations of atheists, it is possible that our sample differs from all atheists in that they are more active than other atheists in promoting the cause of atheism. However, it should be pointed out that not all of the organizations we contacted had an agenda of the promotion of atheism or protecting the rights of atheists. Some of them were merely organizations that attempted to meet the social needs of atheists. Thus it would be inaccurate to categorize our sample as atheists "activists," although it is fair to assume that atheists who are activists in the areas we studied have a higher likelihood of being included in our sample than other atheists.

10. We are certain that many of our respondents will disagree with our contention that atheism is a religious belief. We make this argument since it is a belief about supernaturalism or the lack thereof. As we will see, many atheists view their lack of belief in the supernatural merely as a logical outcome of their assessment of the available data. Yet none of the atheists in our sample claim to be able to prove the nonexistence of the supernatural. Thus, at some point they must make a decision to "believe" that the supernatural does not exist, and we argue that such a belief is by definition religious in nature.

11. Indeed, a common theme among many atheists was their assertion that they can be "good without God."

12. Liston Pope, *Millhands and Preachers* (New Haven, CT: Yale University Press, 1942); H. Richard Niebuhr, *The Social Sources of Denominationalism* (New York: Meridian Books, 1957); Keith A. Roberts and David Yamane, *Religion in Sociological Perspective*, 5th ed. (Los Angeles: Sage, 2012).

13. To put this in a proper context, according to Kosmin and Keysar, *American Religious Identification Survey*, at least 81.6 percent of Americans believe in either a personal God or a higher power.

14. We contend that the value of rationality is one that is highly prized by atheists. However, we should not be surprised that rationality is a value accepted by atheists. Some of our earlier work on cultural progressive activists identified rationality as an important value of that subculture. That research also documented that atheists are overrepresented among cultural progressive activists. George Yancey and David Williamson, *What Motivates Cultural Progressives? Understanding Opposition to the Political and Christian Right* (Waco, TX: Baylor University Press, 2012).

15. Bertrand Russell, "Is There a God?" *Illustrated Magazine*, 1952. He argues that we have no more evidence that there is a God out in the universe than there is that an unseen teapot circles the earth.

4. THE FOOLISHNESS OF RELIGION

1. George Yancey and David A. Williamson, *What Motivates Cultural Progressives? Understanding Opposition to the Political and Christian Right* (Waco, TX: Baylor University Press, 2012).

2. Higher criticism is a critique of the Bible that is done from a basis of literary analysis. This analysis is used to assess the most likely authorship of biblical text, the time it was written, and the location. The assertion of much of higher criticism is that traditional assertions of authorship, timing, and location are incorrect. As such, the Bible is seen as a humanly written book and not divinely inspired.

3. In fact, one of the important spokesmen for atheism, Richard Dawkins, is famous for his adherence to scientism, or the notion that science can explain all aspects of reality. Given that such a prominent atheist promotes this philosophy, it is not surprising that some atheists would also perpetuate the notion of science as the only real explanation of reality.

4. For example, check out Michael O. Emerson and Christian Smith, *Divided by Faith: Evangelical Religion and the Problem of Race in America* (Oxford: Oxford University Press, 2000), as they document the use of free-will individualism by white evangelicals as a way to frame their social understanding. Such free-will individualism is connected to a more conservative political philosophy that is counter to the political understanding of most atheists.

5. PROGRESSIVE POLITICS AS A TENET OF ATHEISM

1. B. Norrander and C. Wilcox, "The Gender Gap in Ideology," *Political Behavior* 30 (2008); G. C. Layman, "Religion and Political Behavior in the United States: The Impact of Beliefs, Affiliations and Commitment from 1980 to 1994," *Public Opinion Quarterly* 61, no. 2 (1997); S. T. Rinehart and J. Perkins, "The Intersection of Gender Politics and Religious Beliefs," *Political Behavior* 11, no. 1 (1989).

2. Michael O. Emerson and Christian Smith, *Divided by Faith: Evangelical Religion and the Problem of Race in America* (Oxford: Oxford University Press, 2000).

3. Kay Deaux et al., "Parameters of Social Identity," *Journal of Personality and Social Psychology* 68, no. 2 (1995); Dominic Abrams, "Political Distinctiveness: An Identity Optimis-

ing Approach," *European Journal of Social Psychology* 24, no. 3 (2006); Leonie Huddy, "From Social to Political Identity: A Critical Examination of Social Identity Theory," *Political Psychology* 22, no. 1 (2001).

4. Barry A. Kosmin et al., "American Nones: The Profile of the No Religion Population, A Report Based on the American Religious Identification Survey 2008," in *Faculty Scholarship* (Hartford, CT: Trinity College, 2009); Bruce E. Hunsberger and Bob Altemeyer, *Atheists: A Groundbreaking Study of America's Nonbelievers* (Amherst, NY: Prometheus Books, 2006).

5. Bob Altemeyer, *Enemies of Freedom: Understanding Right-Wing Authoritarianism* (San Francisco: Jossey-Bass, 1988); Wade C. Rowatt and Lewis M. Franklin, "Christian Orthodoxy, Religious Fundamentalism, and Right-Wing Authoritarianism as Predictors of Implicit Racial Prejudice," *International Journal for the Psychology of Religion* 14, no. 2 (2009).

6. It is of interest that many respondents described churches as just that: a business. For them, the churches did not merit the dignity of being true nonprofits but were merely yet another way in which entrepreneurs are able to make money. In this way they desacralize the meaning of religious organizations and reduce them to just another structural element.

7. James L. Guth and John C. Green, "The Moralizing Minority: Christian Right Support among Political Contributors," in *Religion and the Culture Wars: Dispatches from the Front*, ed. John C. Green (Lanham, MD: Rowman & Littlefield, 1996); Carrie R. Wickham, *Mobilizing Islam: Religion, Activism, and Political Change in Egypt* (New York: Columbia University Press, 2002); Fredrick C. Harris, *Something Within: Religion in African-American Political Activism* (Cambridge: Cambridge University Press, 1999); Steven A. Peterson, "Church Participation and Political Participation: The Spillover Effect," *American Political Research* 20, no. 1 (1992).

6. TOWARD AN ATHEIST MORALITY

1. David Limbaugh, *Persecution: How Liberals Are Waging War against Christianity* (New York: Harper Paperbacks, 2004); Mark R. Levin, *Liberty and Tyranny: A Conservative Manifesto* (Roseburg, OR: Threshold Editions, 2010); Donald Wildmon, *Speechless: Silencing the Christians* (Minneapolis, MN: Richard Vigilante Books, 2009); David Kupelian, *The Marketing of Evil: How Radicals, Elitists, and Pseudo-experts Sell Us Corruption Disguised as Freedom* (Medford, OR: WND Books, 2005).

2. For example, Albert Camus struggled to find meaning in a material world devoid of the supernatural, which he labeled "absurd." He came to the conclusion that we have to accept the absurdity of life. Friedrich Nietzsche declared, "God is dead"—thus we had to find the willpower to develop our morality without reliance on the supernatural. There is a tradition of classic atheist philosophers who struggle with how to make meaning in a life without the supernatural. However, this seems less of a concern in many of the recent "angry" atheist writings.

3. George Yancey and David A. Williamson, *The Cultural War Blues: Cultural Progressives in the United States* (Waco, TX: Baylor University Press, 2012).

4. It is not unrealistic to think that much of this concern has developed because Richard Dawkins in *The God Delusion* (Boston: Houghton Mifflin, 2006) equates religious training with child abuse. As we have noted before, atheists tend to value reading and common literature as a way in which values are communicated to them as a group.

5. We observed relatively little demonizing among our interview participants. We speculate that it is easier to engage in such practices in an online venue since a respondent can remain anonymous. It is likely that social desirability effects are less prevalent with the online survey as it concerns the deep emotional feelings atheists have toward people of faith. If this is true, then gaining an honest emotional assessment of an out-group may be one of the ways in which online methodology is superior to face-to-face interviewing.

6. Penny Edgell, Joseph Gerteis, and Douglass Hartmann, "Atheists as 'Other': Moral Boundaries and Cultural Membership in American Society," *American Sociological Review* 71

(2006); George Yancey, "Who Has Religious Prejudice? Differing Sources of Anti-Religious Animosity in the United States," *Review of Religious Research* 52, no. 2 (2010).

7. ATHEISM IN THE UNITED STATES

1. Gavin Hyman, "Atheism in Modern History," in *The Cambridge Companion to Atheism*, ed. Michael Martin (Cambridge: Cambridge University Press, 2007); Gavin Hyman, *A Short History of Atheism* (London: I.B. Tauris, 2010).

2. Frank Newport, "More Than 9 in 10 Americans Continue to Believe in God," www.gallup.com, 2011.

3. In the 1944 poll the question was worded, "Do you, personally, believe in a God?"

4. Bruce E. Hunsberger and Bob Altemeyer, *Atheists: A Groundbreaking Study of America's Nonbelievers* (Amherst, NY: Prometheus Books, 2006).

5. Barry A. Kosmin et al., "American Nones: The Profile of the No Religion Population, A Report Based on the American Religious Identification Survey 2008," in *Faculty Scholarship* (Hartford, CT: Trinity College, 2009).

6. Bob Altemeyer and Bruce Hunsberger, *Amazing Conversions: Why Some Turn to Faith & Others Abandon Religion* (Amherst, NY: Prometheus Books, 1997).

7. Hunsberger and Altemeyer, *Atheists*, 18–19.

8. Penny Edgell, Joseph Gerteis, and Douglas Hartmann, "Atheists as 'Other': Moral Boundaries and Cultural Membership in American Society," *American Sociological Review* 71, no. 2 (April 2006).

9. Emile Durkheim believed that one source for the God concept was the abstracted representation that people have and use as an expression of their veneration of society.

10. Hyman, *A Short History of Atheism*, 6–7.

11. Richard Hofstadter, *Anti-intellectualism in American Life* (New York: Vintage, 1963).

12. Edgell, Gerteis, and Hartmann, "Atheists as 'Other.'"

13. Newport, "More Than 9 in 10 Americans Continue to Believe in God."

14. This also is the time when pluralism had an even deeper impact on the forms and practice of religion than ever before. Pluralism is nice on the surface—we agree to disagree and get on with our daily lives—but in fact pluralism leads to relativism and the exclusion of absolute belief in any one particular religion. Peter L. Berger in *A Far Glory: The Quest for Faith in an Age of Credulity* (New York: Free Press, 1992) describes it as painful, with no clear alternative where one can rest absolute beliefs on anything. Perhaps the alternative for many who experienced this was either to believe in nothing or to retreat to absolute beliefs and fundamentalism.

15. Peter L. Berger, *The Heretical Imperative: Contemporary Possibilities of Religious Affirmation* (New York: Anchor Press, 1979).

16. A recent example captures this idea. The Roman Catholic Church, primarily through its American bishops, denounced a proposed new policy that would require all health care providers to offer women's services, including contraception. That would have included Catholic hospitals, therefore forcing Catholic institutions to do what the Church formally prohibited. However, one study, Rachel K. Jones and Joerg Dreweke's *Countering Conventional Wisdom: New Evidence on Religion and Contraceptive Use* (New York: Guttmacher Institute, 2011), claims that more than 90 percent of Roman Catholic women have used birth control. We suggest, as have others, that knowing that someone is Catholic or Baptist or Episcopalian really does not tell us much about their theological or ethical or even moral orientations at all.

17. Michael Lienesch, *In the Beginning: Fundamentalism, the Scopes Trial, and the Making of the Antievolution Movement* (Chapel Hill: University of North Carolina Press, 2007).

18. The National Cathedral in Washington, DC, which is used for many solemn state events, is in fact an Episcopalian cathedral.

19. www.episcopalchurch.org.

20. BBC News, July 15, 2008. Statistics from Anglican Church official statistics.

21. These numbers reflect the people who are on Anglican and Episcopal Church rolls and are not necessarily regular attenders.

22. We assume the discrepancy between this figure and that stated earlier from Gallup polls has to do with the wording of the questions. Gallup in 2011 asked, "Do you believe in God?" In 1944 Gallup asked, "Do you, personally, believe in God?" The *American Religious Identification Survey* asked, "Do you believe in a personal God?" The first two don't seem to have made much of a difference. The issue of a "personal God," however, may mean that some who believe in God actually believe in deism's God, who is not personal.

23. Kosmin et al., "American Nones."

24. Ronald L. Johnstone, *Religion in Society: A Sociology of Religion*, 8th ed. (Upper Saddle River, NJ: Prentice Hall, 2007).

25. Hunsberger and Altemeyer, *Atheists*, 75.

26. George Yancey, *Interracial Contact and Social Change* (Boulder, CO: Lynne Rienner, 2007).

27. Gordon Gauchat, "Politicization of Science in the Public Sphere: A Study of Public Trust in the United States, 1974 to 2010," *American Sociological Review* 77, no. 2 (2012): 182.

28. Peter L. Berger, *Facing up to Modernity* (New York: Basic Books, 1977).

29. Altemeyer and Hunsberger, *Amazing Conversions*, 15.

30. Hyman, *A Short History of Atheism*, 83.

31. We have chosen, at this point, not to go into a deeper exploration of epistemology here. We should mention, though, that religious scholars have pointed to the error of insistence on scientific proof in certain kinds of inquiry. For example, court cases are decided every day by the preponderance of evidence, none of which may be strictly scientific. In a court of law the arguments made are based on logic, probability, association, and so forth.

32. Paul DiMaggio, John Evans, and Bethany Bryson, "Have Americans' Social Attitudes Become More Polarized?" *American Journal of Sociology* 102, no. 3 (1996).

8. SUMMARY AND CONCLUSION

1. Gavin Hyman, "Atheism in Modern History," in *The Cambridge Companion to Atheism*, ed. Michael Martin (Cambridge: Cambridge University Press, 2007).

2. Mark Juergensmeyer, *Terror in the Mind of God* (Berkeley: University of California Press, 2000).

3. We are fully aware of the long and complex history of the various Christian approaches to soteriology. Rather than reviewing all of the issues of faith, works, grace, denominational affiliation, and any other basis of salvation that has been argued by Christian denominations, we have chosen to use an ideal type of traditional notions of salvation.

4. George Yancey, *Interracial Contact and Social Change* (Boulder, CO: Lynne Rienner, 2007).

5. Bruce E. Hunsberger and Bob Altemeyer, *Atheists: A Groundbreaking Study of America's Nonbelievers* (Amherst, NY: Prometheus Books, 2006).

6. Pew Forum on Religion & Public Life, "Not All Nonbelievers Call Themselves Atheists," http://www.pewforum.org/Not-All-Nonbelievers-Call-Themselves-Atheists.aspx (April 2, 2009).

7. Bob Altemeyer and Bruce Hunsberger, *Amazing Conversions: Why Some Turn to Faith & Others Abandon Religion* (Amherst, NY: Prometheus Books, 1997).

Bibliography

Altemeyer, Bob, and Bruce Hunsberger. *Amazing Conversions: Why Some Turn to Faith & Others Abandon Religion*. Amherst, NY: Prometheus Books, 1997.

American Atheists. www.atheists.org (May 21, 2012).

Bainbridge, William S. "Atheism." *Interdisciplinary Journal of Research on Religion* 1 (January 2005): 1–24.

Barbour, Ian G. *Religion and Science: Historical and Contemporary Issues*. San Francisco: HarperSanFrancisco, 1997.

Barker, Dan. *Godless: How an Evangelical Preacher Became One of America's Leading Atheists*. Berkeley, CA: Ulysses Press, 2008.

Berger, Peter L. *Facing Up to Modernity*. New York: Basic Books, 1977.

———. *A Far Glory: The Quest for Faith in an Age of Credulity*. New York: Free Press, 1992.

———. *The Heretical Imperative: Contemporary Possibilities of Religious Affirmation*. New York: Anchor Press, 1979.

———. *Pyramids of Sacrifice: Political Ethics and Social Change*. Garden City, NY: Anchor Books, 1976.

Bremmer, Jan N. "Atheism in Antiquity." In *The Cambridge Companion to Atheism*, edited by Michael Martin, 11–26. Cambridge: Cambridge University Press, 2007.

Carter, Stephen L. *The Culture of Disbelief: How American Law and Politics Trivialize Religious Devotion*. New York: Basic Books, 1993.

Clayton, Philip. *God and Contemporary Science*. Grand Rapids, MI: Wm. B. Eerdmans, 1997.

Dawkins, Richard. *The God Delusion*. Boston: Mariner Books, 2006.

DeJean, Joan. *Ancients against Moderns: Culture Wars and the Making of a Fin de Siècle*. Chicago: University of Chicago Press, 1997.

DiMaggio, Paul, John Evans, and Bethany Bryson. "Have Americans' Social Attitudes Become More Polarized?" *American Journal of Sociology* 102, no. 3 (1996): 690–755.

Durkheim, Emile. *The Elementary Forms of the Religious Life*. New York: George Allen & Unwin, 1915.

Edgell, Penny, Joseph Gerteis, and Douglas Hartmann. "Atheists as 'Other': Moral Boundaries and Cultural Membership in American Society." *American Sociological Review* 71 (April 2006): 211–34.

Ensey, Caydee. "Students Attend Inaugural Reason Rally." *North Texas Daily*, March 27, 2012.

Eusebius. *The Ecclesiastical History of Eusebius Pamphilus*. Translated by Christian Frederick Cruse. Grand Rapids, MI: Baker Book House, 1955.

Fudge, Edward William. *The Fire That Consumes: A Biblical and Historical Study of the Doctrine of Final Punishment*. Lincoln, NE: iUniverse.com, 2001.

Gauchat, Gordon. "Politicization of Science in the Public Sphere: A Study of Public Trust in the United States, 1974 to 2010. *American Sociological Review* 77, no. 2 (2012): 167–87.

Gibbs, Jack P. *Control: Sociology's Central Notion.* Urbana: University of Illinois Press, 1989.

Hadaway, C. Kirk. "Denominational Switching and Religiosity." *Review of Religious Research* 21, no. 4 (1980): 451–61.

Haught, James A. *2000 Years of Disbelief: Famous People with the Courage to Doubt.* Amherst, NY: Prometheus Books, 1996.

Hecht, Jennifer Michael, *Doubt: A History.* New York: Harper, 2006.

Hitchens, Christopher. *God Is Not Great: How Religion Poisons Everything.* New York: Twelve Hatchette Book Group, 2007.

Hofstadter, Richard. *Anti-intellectualism in American Life.* New York: Vintage, 1963.

Hoge, Dean R., Benton Johnson, and Donald Al Luidens. "Types of Denominational Switching among Protestant Young Adults." *Journal for the Scientific Study of Religion* 34, no. 2 (1995): 253–58.

Hunsberger, Bruce, and Bob Altemeyer. *Atheists: A Groundbreaking Study of America's Nonbelievers.* Amherst, NY: Prometheus Books, 2006.

Hunter, James Davison. *Culture Wars: The Struggle to Define America.* New York: Basic Books, 1991.

Hyman, Gavin. "Atheism in Modern History." In *The Cambridge Companion to Atheism*, edited by Michael Martin, 27–46. Cambridge: Cambridge University Press, 2007.

———. *A Short History of Atheism.* London: I.B. Tauris, 2010.

Jackson, John G. "Hubert Henry Harrison: The Black Socrates." http://atheists.org/content/hubert-henry-harrison-black-socrates.

Johnstone, Ronald L. *Religion in Society: A Sociology of Religion.* Eighth edition. Upper Saddle River, NJ: Prentice Hall, 2007.

Jones, Rachel K., and Joerg Dreweke. *Countering Conventional Wisdom: New Evidence on Religion and Contraceptive Use.* New York: Guttmacher Institute, 2011.

Juergensmeyer, Mark. *Terror in the Mind of God: The Global Rise of Religious Violence.* Berkeley: University of California Press, 2000.

Kelley, Dean M. *Why Conservative Churches Are Growing: A Study in Sociology.* New York: Harper & Row, 1972.

Kosmin, Barry A., and Ariela Keysar. *American Religious Identification Survey: Summary Report.* Hartford, CT: Trinity College, 2009.

Lienesch, Michael. *In the Beginning: Fundamentalism, the Scopes Trial, and the Making of the Antievolution Movement.* Chapel Hill: University of North Carolina Press, 2007.

Loveland, Matthew T. "Religious Switching: Preference Development, Maintenance, and Change." *Journal for the Scientific Study of Religion* 42, no. 1 (2003): 147–57.

Martin, Michael. *Atheism: A Philosophical Justification.* Philadelphia: Temple University Press, 1990.

———, ed. *The Cambridge Companion to Atheism.* Cambridge: Cambridge University Press, 2007.

Nall, Jeff. "Fundamentalist Atheism and Its Intellectual Failures." *Humanity and Society* 32 (August 2008): 263–80.

Numbers, Ronald L. *Darwinism Comes to America.* Cambridge, MA: Harvard University Press, 1998.

O'Hair, Madalyn Murray. "History of Atheism." *American Rationalist* 17 (1962), http://atheists.org/content/history-atheism.

Pew Forum on Religion & Public Life. "Not All Nonbelievers Call Themselves Atheists." http://www.pewforum.org/Not-All-Nonbelievers-Call-Themselves-Atheists.aspx (April 2, 2009).

Polkinghorne, John. *Belief in God in an Age of Science.* New Haven, CT: Yale University Press, 2003.

Ross, Hugh. *The Creator and the Cosmos: How the Greatest Scientific Discoveries of the Century Reveal God.* Colorado Springs, CO: NavPress, 1993.

Sherkat, Darren E. "Beyond Belief: Atheism, Agnosticism, and Theistic Certainty in the United States." *Sociological Spectrum* 28 (2008): 438–59.

Stark, Rodney, and Roger Finke. *Acts of Faith: Explaining the Human Side of Religion*. Berkeley: University of California Press, 2000.

Stenger, Victor J. *The New Atheism: Taking a Stand for Science and Reason*. Amherst, NY: Prometheus Books, 2009.

Thrower, James. *Western Atheism: A Short History*. Amherst, NY: Prometheus Books, 2000.

Weber, Max. *The Protestant Ethic and the Spirit of Capitalism*. London: Unwin Paperbacks, 1930/1985.

———. *The Theory of Social and Economic Organization*. New York: Oxford University Press, 1947.

Yancey, George. *Interracial Contact and Social Change*. Boulder, CO: Lynne Rienner, 2007.

Zeitlin, Irving M. *The Religious Experience: Classical Philosophical and Social Theories*. Upper Saddle River, NJ: Pearson Press, 2004.

Zuckerman, Phil. "Atheism: Contemporary Numbers and Patterns." In *The Cambridge Companion to Atheism*, edited by Michael Martin, 47–68. Cambridge: Cambridge University Press, 2007.

Index

abortion, 1, 5, 66, 111, 131n3, 133n2
American Civil Liberties Union (ACLU), 29
African Americans, 5, 12, 65, 77, 130n22
agnostics, 2, 23, 25, 34, 119, 121
American Atheists (organization), 30
American Revolution, 24
Americans United for the Separation of Church and State, 30, 96
Anglican Church, 11, 103–104, 105, 106
apostasy, 100, 105, 110, 122
Apostle Paul, 21–22
Aquinas, Thomas, 22, 23, 120
Aristotelian philosophers, 23
atheistic philosophers, 86, 101, 135n2

Baylor Religious Studies, 39
Bible, 12, 27, 28, 55, 102–103, 108, 110, 120, 134n2
Bible Belt, 14, 15, 108–109, 114, 119, 122
brainwashing, 92, 93, 117

Catholics, 4, 6, 7, 10, 11, 23, 26, 101, 115, 118, 121, 131n42, 136n16
Christian Coalition, 30
Christian Right, 28, 34, 57, 133n3
Christian theology, 22–23
coming out as atheist, 6, 17, 107
conservatism, 28, 96, 116; Anglican, 105; Christian, 10, 12, 17, 19, 28, 34, 100, 110, 112, 113, 117, 118–119, 120, 121,

122, 123, 131n3; political, 14, 65, 66, 67, 74, 79, 107, 108, 110, 111–112; religious, 4–5, 12, 15, 27, 28, 31, 93, 105, 106, 108, 110, 112, 115, 116, 120, 121
contact hypothesis, 15, 16, 99, 108, 109, 114, 119–120
contraception, 131n42, 136n16
control, 7, 9–13, 14, 16, 31, 67, 76, 85, 99, 103, 106, 114, 116, 118, 119, 122; religious, 5, 8, 20, 21, 23–24, 29, 71, 79

Darwinism, 13, 25, 26, 27, 28, 115, 116
Defense of Marriage Act, 10
Democrats, 107, 112
discrimination, 6, 130n22
doubt, 7–8, 25; in atheists, 36, 44–45
Duns Scotus, John, 9, 22, 24, 111, 132n13

education, 20, 30, 43, 75, 88, 89, 90, 108, 109, 118; scientific, 117
educational institutions, 14, 77, 78, 80
the Enlightenment, 8, 24
evangelicals, 1, 8, 14, 15, 16, 19, 49, 106, 108, 119

Falwell, Jerry, 17
Freedom from Religion Foundation, 8, 30, 96, 107
French philosophers, 27, 30
French Revolution, 24, 27

fundamentalists, 6, 11, 26, 100, 105, 106, 107–108, 111, 116, 121, 122; atheist, 1, 4, 6
The Fundamentals, 28

Greek philosophers, 20, 115

higher criticism, 28, 55, 134n2
homophobia, 117
homosexuals, 6, 29, 102, 104, 133n2
humanism, 4, 12, 16, 23, 29, 113, 114, 117, 118
Hyman, Gavin, 1, 8, 9, 22, 23, 113

immigrants, 6, 117
immorality, 17, 27, 28, 68, 90, 91, 94, 110
income, 39, 109
irrationality, 40, 46, 47, 49–53, 57, 61, 63, 76, 87, 91
irreligiosity, 8, 12, 27, 100

Jews/Jewish, 23, 26, 115, 118, 121; history, 18, 21; Orthodox, 121

McCarthyism, 28
morality, 16, 26, 27, 67, 68, 85–97, 103, 110, 114, 116–117, 118, 120, 123, 135n2; definition, 85; political, 86
Moral Majority, 17, 30

natural philosophers, 20
natural theology, 22

particularism, 49, 58, 63, 65, 68, 76, 91
People for the American Way, 30
progressives, 9, 10, 15, 24, 27, 29, 30, 31, 96, 103, 105, 107, 116, 117, 118; cultural, 34, 49, 79, 93, 97, 133n2, 134n14; ideologies of, 18, 26–27, 28,

86, 104, 116, 117; political, 5, 63, 65–82, 95, 109, 111–112; religious, 2, 4–5, 28, 100, 102–103, 104, 105, 106, 115, 120, 130n18
Protestant Reformation, 10, 23–24, 118, 131n40

race, 27, 109
racism, 5, 12, 117
rationality, 5, 8, 10, 11, 12, 16, 20, 23, 24, 46, 47, 54, 57, 61, 63, 65, 68, 95, 96, 101, 103, 104, 115, 118, 134n14
Republicans, 17, 107, 112
Robertson, Pat, 17

same-sex marriage, 1, 66, 67, 104, 112, 131n3
science, 4, 5, 7, 8, 9, 11, 12, 14, 17, 22–23, 24–25, 26, 29, 44, 52, 57–59, 60, 89, 90, 101–102, 103, 104, 109–111, 112, 113, 115, 116, 117, 118, 119, 121; natural, 19; social, 118
secularization hypothesis, 3, 27
secular society, 80, 86, 87, 89, 90, 94–95, 96
separation of church and state, 1, 5, 9–10, 13, 14, 25–26, 27, 29, 30, 78–79, 88, 104, 116
sexism, 14, 116, 117
sexual revolution, 102
socialization, 117, 118; religious, 63, 109
stem-cell research, 66

teapot argument, 46–47, 134n15
theocracy, 5, 79, 105, 109, 119

women, 26, 29, 103, 104, 117, 130n22, 131n42, 131n3, 136n16; liberation, 6, 102